GROWING
IN CHRIST

VICTORY SERIES

STUDY 5

GROWING
IN CHRIST

DEEPEN YOUR
RELATIONSHIP WITH JESUS

NEIL T. ANDERSON

BETHANY HOUSE
a division of Baker Publishing Group
www.BethanyHouse.com

Published by Bethany House Publishers
11400 Hampshire Avenue South
Bloomington, Minnesota 55438
www.bethanyhouse.com

Bethany House Publishers is a division of
Baker Publishing Group, Grand Rapids, Michigan

Printed in the United States of America

Library of Congress Control Number: 2014958630

ISBN 978-0-7642-1702-9

Cover design by Rob Williams, InsideOutCreativeArts

15   16   17   18   19   20   21   7   6   5   4   3   2   1

Contents

Contents

Introduction

The Victory Series

S o then, just as you received Christ Jesus as Lord, continue to live your lives in him, rooted and built up in him, strengthened in the faith as you were taught" (Colossians 2:6–7). Paul's New Covenant theology is based on who we are "in Christ." As a believer in Christ, you must first be rooted "in Him" so you can be built up "in Him." Just as you encounter challenges as you grow physically, you will encounter hurdles as you grow spiritually. The following chart illustrates what obstacles you need to overcome and lessons you need to learn at various stages of growth spiritually, rationally, emotionally, volitionally, and relationally.

Levels of Conflict

	Level One Rooted in Christ	**Level Two** Built up in Christ	**Level Three** Living in Christ
Spiritual	Lack of salvation or assurance (Eph. 2:1–3)	Living according to the flesh (Gal. 5:19–21)	Insensitive to the Spirit's leading (Heb. 5:11–14)
Rational	Pride and ignorance (1 Cor. 8:1)	Wrong belief or philosophy (Col. 2:8)	Lack of knowledge (Hos. 4:6)
Emotional	Fearful, guilty, and shameful (Matt. 10:26–33; Rom. 3:23)	Angry, anxious, and depressed (Eph. 4:31; 1 Pet. 5:7; 2 Cor. 4:1–18)	Discouraged and sorrowful (Gal. 6:9)

	Level One Rooted in Christ	**Level Two** Built up in Christ	**Level Three** Living in Christ
Volitional	Rebellious (1 Tim. 1:9)	Lack of self-control (1 Cor. 3:1–3)	Undisciplined (2 Thess. 3:7, 11)
Relational	Rejected and unloved (1 Pet. 2:4)	Bitter and unforgiving (Col. 3:13)	Selfish (1 Cor. 10:24; Phil. 2:1–5)

WILL (handwritten annotation pointing to Volitional)

This VICTORY SERIES will address these obstacles and hurdles and help you understand what it means to be firmly rooted in Christ, grow in Christ, live free in Christ, and overcome in Christ. The goal of the course is to help you attain greater levels of spiritual growth, as the following diagram illustrates:

Levels of Growth

	Level One Rooted in Christ	**Level Two** Built up in Christ	**Level Three** Living in Christ
Spiritual	Child of God (Rom. 8:16)	Lives according to the Spirit (Gal. 5:22–23)	Led by the Spirit (Rom. 8:14)
Rational	Knows the truth (John 8:32)	Correctly uses the Bible (2 Tim. 2:15)	Adequate and equipped (2 Tim. 3:16–17)
Emotional	Free (Gal. 5:1)	Joyful, peaceful, and patient (Gal. 5:22)	Contented (Phil. 4:11)
Volitional	Submissive (Rom. 13:1–5)	Self-controlled (Gal. 5:23)	Disciplined (1 Tim. 4:7–8)
Relational	Accepted and forgiven (Rom. 5:8; 15:7)	Forgiving (Eph. 4:32)	Loving and unselfish (Phil. 2:1–5)

God's Story for You and *Your New Identity*, the first two studies in the VICTORY SERIES, focused on the issues that help the believer become firmly rooted in Christ (level one in above chart). If you have completed those studies, then you know the whole gospel, who you are in Christ, and who your heavenly Father is. The two subsequent studies—*Your Foundation in Christ* and *Renewing Your Mind*—and this study, *Growing in Christ*, discuss issues related to your spiritual growth (level two in the above chart). *Growing in Christ* provides the transition from level two to level three by offering help for those who have lingering addictive behaviors.

8

As you work through the six sessions in this Bible study, you will learn how to receive God's wisdom and discernment, use your spiritual gifts appropriately, grow through marital and familial relationships, overcome sexual bondage and chemical addiction, and understand the truth behind why each of us suffers. The Steps to Freedom in Christ will be mentioned during this study. This booklet can be purchased at any Christian bookstore or from Freedom in Christ Ministries. The Steps to Freedom in Christ is a process that can help you resolve your personal and spiritual conflicts through genuine repentance and faith in God. The theology and application of the Steps is explained in the book *Discipleship Counseling*.

Before starting each daily reading, review the portion of Scripture listed for that day, then complete the questions at the end of each day's reading. These questions have been written to allow you to reflect on the material and apply to your life the ideas presented in the reading. At the end of each study, I have included a quote from a Church father illustrating the continuity of the Christian faith. Featured articles will appear in the text throughout the series, which are for the edification of the reader and not necessarily meant for discussion.

If you are part of a small group, be prepared to share your thoughts and insights with your group. You may also want to set up an accountability partnership with someone in your group to encourage you as you apply what you have learned in each session. For those of you who are leading a small group, there are leader tips at the end of this book that will help you guide your participants through the material.

As with any spiritual discipline, you will be tempted at times not to finish this study. There is a "sure reward" for those who make a "sure commitment." The VICTORY SERIES is far more than an intellectual exercise. The truth will not set you free if you only acknowledge it and discuss it on an intellectual level. For the truth to transform your life, you must believe it personally and allow it to sink deep into your heart. Trust the Holy Spirit to lead you into all truth and enable you to be the person God has created you to be. Decide to live what you have chosen to believe.

Dr. Neil T. Anderson

9

Spiritual Discernment

A primary dictum of the Western theological tradition, channeled through the conduit of Augustine and Anselm, had been that faith led to understanding. This was a faith in Christ grounded in personal self-awareness of sin, cognizant of the continual lure of self-deception, rooted in the intrinsic authority of Scripture and the divinely inspired revelation it communicated, and nurtured by the Church's history of reflection on the meaning of God's Word to humanity.

The Enlightenment perspective stood this approach on its head. Understanding would lead to a mature faith, rather than the reverse. Hence, those aspects of the Christian tradition that failed to meet the standards of human reason—liberated, autonomous reason—were regarded with suspicion and for many ultimately discarded. Is it surprising that the resurrection, incarnation, Trinity, miracles and other revelatory gifts soon became negotiables?[1]

—Christopher Hall, *Reading Scriptures With the Church Fathers*

Daily Readings

1. Our First Line of Defense	1 Kings 3:5–15
2. Discerning Good and Evil	Hebrews 5:12–6:3
3. Listening to God	John 10:1–30
4. Spiritual Disclosure	John 16:5–15
5. Spiritual Wisdom	1 Corinthians 2:6–16

1

Our First Line of Defense

1 Kings 3:5–15

Key Point

The Holy Spirit bears witness with our spirit and enables us to know right from wrong in the spiritual realm.

Key Verses

I will ask the Father, and he will give you another advocate to help you and be with you forever—the Spirit of truth. The world cannot accept him, because it neither sees him nor knows him. But you know him, for he lives with you and will be in you.

John 14:16–17

In a world saturated with deceiving spirits, false prophets, and false teachers, the need for believers to exercise discernment cannot be overstated. In the Old Testament, the Hebrew verb *bin* and its variations—translated as "discern," "distinguish," and "understand"—are used 247 times. The word means "to make a distinction, or separate from." The New Testament Greek counterpart, *diakrino*, also means "to separate or divide." The use of the word is applied primarily to judging or making decisions.

The Holy Spirit enables us to distinguish right from wrong, truth from lies, and God's thoughts from humankind's thoughts.

As believers, we think with our minds, but we discern with our spirits. Mentally we can know whether something is right or wrong in the natural realm by observation and inquiry. Theologically, we can agree or disagree with a verbal or written statement based on our education, experience, and understanding of God's Word. However, the spiritual world is not always discernible by our natural senses. To chart our way in the spiritual world requires the presence of God.

When the Holy Spirit takes up residence in our lives, He bears witness with our spirit and enables us to know right from wrong in the spiritual realm. This God-given ability to discern is like a sixth sense that enables us to know that something is right or wrong, even though we may not know intellectually what is right or what is wrong.

In the Bible, the interaction between God and Solomon is helpful in understanding spiritual discernment. David had died and Solomon had taken his place as king of Israel. Solomon loved the Lord, but by his own admission, he was too young and inexperienced to be the king: "Now, Lord my God, you have made your servant king in place of my father David. But I am only a little child and do not know how to carry out my duties" (1 Kings 3:7). The Lord appeared to Solomon during the night in a dream and said, "Ask for whatever you want me to give you" (verse 5). Solomon asked God for "a discerning heart to govern your people and to distinguish between right and wrong" (verse 9). The Lord was pleased with Solomon's request.

This passage reveals two key concepts about discernment. First, God gave Solomon the ability to discern because his motives were pure. Solomon wasn't asking for a wise and discerning heart for his own personal profit, or even to gain an advantage over his enemies. He wanted discernment in order to administer justice and know good from evil. Motive is crucial, because the power to discern can be misused in the Church. It is a powerful advantage to know something no one else knows.

Second, spiritual discernment is always concerned with the moral realm of good and evil. The Holy Spirit gives us a check in our spirit when something is wrong. Discernment is our first line of defense when our natural

14

senses aren't able to register any danger or direction. However, the ability to discern spiritually does not negate the necessity of knowing God's Word. We should always be like the Bereans who "received the message with great eagerness and examined the Scriptures every day to see if what Paul said was true" (Acts 17:11).

What is the meaning of the word "discernment"? Why is it critical for believers to exercise discernment?

_____

_____

_____

What role does the Holy Spirit play in our spiritual discernment?

_____

_____

_____

Why did God grant Solomon's request for a wise and discerning heart?

_____

_____

_____

If you don't sense a peace about a decision, or a place, or the presence of others, how should you proceed?

_____

_____

_____

How can you practice discernment and learn to trust such impressions?

_____

_____

_____

I am of the opinion that every rational creature—without distinction—receives a share of [the Holy Spirit] in the same way as of the Wisdom and of the Word of God. I observe, however, that the chief coming of the Holy Spirit is declared to men after the ascension of Christ to heaven—rather than before His coming into the world. Before that, the gift of the Holy Spirit was conferred upon the prophets alone and upon a few individuals.

Origen (AD 184–253)

2

Discerning Good and Evil

Hebrews 5:12–6:3

Key Point

Mature Christians should share their discernment that something is wrong but should not suggest or even hint as to what is wrong without knowing the facts.

Key Verse

But solid food is for the mature, who by constant use have trained themselves to distinguish good from evil.

Hebrews 5:14

In addition to the presence of the Holy Spirit, among the Church's greatest assets are mature saints. They have put their faith into practice and understand the teaching about righteousness. They have had their senses trained to discern good and evil. The Church's greatest liability, however, is saints who have gotten old but haven't matured. They should be able to teach others, but instead they need to be taught the elementary truths of God's Word. These spiritual infants haven't successfully put God's Word into practice. They lack the skills and sensitivity that come from maturity.

Sound doctrine is like a skeleton in the body—it is absolutely essential for stability and structure. However, a skeleton by itself is dead, and so is orthodox teaching without the life of Christ. "The person without the Spirit does not accept the things that come from the Spirit of God but considers them foolishness, and cannot understand them because they are discerned only through the Spirit. The person with the Spirit makes judgments about all things, but such a person is not subject to merely human judgments" (1 Corinthians 2:14–15).

The "elementary teaching" that the writer of Hebrews describes in 5:12–6:3 is what we would call "theological knowledge." Sound doctrine is essential, but learning to walk with God is more than an intellectual exercise. Those who put their faith into practice have trained themselves to distinguish good from evil. Experience is a good teacher if it is combined with a good theology empowered by the Holy Spirit.

Paul makes a similar point in his first letter to the church at Corinth. He wanted to give the Corinthians solid food, but he could only give them milk because they were not able to receive it (see 1 Corinthians 3:1–3). They were not able to receive solid food because of the jealousy and quarrels among them. They were acting like mere humans instead of children of God.

There are many people who cannot receive solid teaching because they have never put into practice what they have learned and have never resolved their personal and spiritual conflicts. Immature saints proceed without caution. They conduct business as usual in the Church, and as a result, the spiritual atmosphere is clouded and members operate in the flesh. The mature saint can sense the oppression and can alert the others while calling for prayer, but spiritually immature saints see no danger.

In the same way, spiritually immature parents see no visible signs that their children are in trouble. Discerning parents know when something is wrong, petition God on behalf of their children, and share their discernment lovingly with their children without judgment. They let their children know that they are aware something is wrong but don't try to guess what is wrong when they don't know. They let the Holy Spirit bring the conviction, keep the communication lines open, and remain available.

Those who are spiritually discerning can sense a false prophet before that prophet's false doctrine is exposed. They can sense a compatible spirit in another believer and discern an incompatible spirit in others. They know during and after an event whether something is their idea or God's idea. They know when they are living by faith in the power of the Holy Spirit and can sense when they aren't.

Why are mature saints such a great asset for the Church? Why are old saints who didn't mature a potential liability for the Church?

What is the function of sound doctrine in our lives? Why is intellectual knowledge not enough by itself to discern good and evil?

What can those who are spiritually discerning detect before the error is exposed?

Have you ever correctly sensed that something was wrong and then guessed incorrectly as to what was wrong? If so, how did that work out for you?

How do you plan on proceeding in the future when you discern something is wrong? What should you do, and what shouldn't you do?

_____

_____

_____

> *The spiritual man gives thanks always for all things to God—by righteous hearing and divine reading, by true investigation, by holy oblation, and by blessed prayer. Always lauding, hymning, blessing, and praising—such a soul is never separated from God at any time.*
>
> Clement of Alexandria (AD 150–215)

3

Listening to God
John 10:1–30

Key Point

God's voice comes with its own authority and enables us to know with confidence what is true and what is right.

Key Verse

The gatekeeper opens the gate for him, and the sheep listen to his voice. He calls his own sheep by name and leads them out.

John 10:3

Jesus said, "My sheep listen to my voice; I know them, and they follow me. I give them eternal life, and they shall never perish; no one will snatch them out of my hand" (John 10:27–28). The security that we have in Christ is not based on our ability to hang on to the hand of God. It is based on God's ability to hold on to us and protect us against the spiritual wolves that would try to snatch us out of His hand.

Jesus is the Great Shepherd, and we are the sheep of His pasture. He calls every one of us by name, and we listen to His voice (see verse 3). "When he has brought out all his own, he goes on ahead of them, and his sheep follow him because they know his voice" (verse 4). On His own authority, Jesus has laid down His life for us. He is not a hired hand who works for wages. He is the Great Shepherd who loves us.

God has spoken through His prophets and apostles, who faithfully proclaimed His Word and wrote it down under the inspiration of the Holy Spirit. We listen to the voice of God when we read His Word and when we hear it proclaimed by faithful servants who have been called as evangelists, pastors, and teachers. We also listened to His voice at salvation when Jesus opened the gate and invited us in. Our acceptance of that invitation may have been in response to a gospel tract or an evangelistic meeting, an invitation at church, or someone who simply shared his or her faith.

However, even though we might have heard the gospel proclaimed or saw it in print, there was an inner "voice" that persuaded us to come inside. We felt convicted of our sin, but at the same time we saw the open door because our eyes had been opened. We knew that somebody was calling us. It probably wasn't audible, but we heard it in our spirit and we responded to the call. Somehow, we knew the truth in a way we had never known before.

The Book of Discipline of the Religious Society of Friends says, "Our power to perceive the light of God is, of all our powers, the one which we need most to cultivate and develop. As exercise strengthens the body and education enlarges the mind, so the spiritual faculty within us grows as we use it in seeing and doing God's will."

We don't always hear with our ears the voice of God, nor do we see with our natural eyes. The spiritual world does not operate through our natural senses; therefore, our knowledge of it is not received through the normal channels of perception. Coupled with the written Word, which is hidden in our hearts, this inner voice nudges us in the right direction or gives us a check in our spirit against that which is wrong. We start thinking thoughts that are wise, insightful, and in accordance with Scripture. Somehow we know what we are supposed to do or say—and with a sense of confidence that is not natural. Inspiration from God comes with its own authority. God is leading us, and we are following Him.

On what basis can we be secure in Christ?

How does the Holy Spirit work within us in conjunction with Scripture?

What are the limitations of our natural senses?

When you "heard" the voice of God calling you to follow Him, how did you know it was God whom you were following?

How can you cultivate the "power to perceive the light of God"?

We know the things which are in the mind of Christ, which He has willed and revealed to us. This does not mean that we know everything which Christ knows but rather that everything which we know comes from Him and is spiritual.

John Chrysostom (AD 347–407)

4

Spiritual Disclosure

John 16:5–15

Key Point

The primary work of the Holy Spirit is to communicate God's presence to us.

Key Verse

All that belongs to the Father is mine. That is why I said the Spirit will receive from me what he will make known to you.

John 16:15

Because of the Holy Spirit within us, we have the power to live the Christian life, but that is not the only work—and not the primary work—of the Holy Spirit. We are never instructed to pursue power, because we already have it (see Ephesians 1:18–19). Our Christian walk is distorted when we pursue things we already have. The Holy Spirit is the divine impetus behind our spiritual gifts, but that also is not the primary work of the Holy Spirit. The church at Corinth seemed to have all the gifts, but they were immature. We are never instructed to seek spiritual gifts for ourselves, but we are instructed to seek the Giver and allow Him to gift us any way He chooses.

The primary work of the Holy Spirit is to communicate God's presence to us. While it was good that Jesus was physically present with the disciples, it was better that He left, so He could be spiritually within every believer through the Holy Spirit. Jesus said, "When [the Holy Spirit] comes, he will prove the world to be in the wrong about sin and righteousness and judgment" (John 16:8). Sin is rebellion against God that reached its climax in the crucifixion of Christ.

The greatest sin is unbelief (see John 3:18), and it is the unique work of the Holy Spirit to convict the world of sin so that people will turn to Christ. The Holy Spirit will bring glory to Jesus by making known within us His resurrection and ascension (see John 16:14). In addition, the Holy Spirit will bear witness to the judgment of Satan. "The prince of this world now stands condemned" (John 16:11). Satan knows that his future is doomed, and he will do all that he can to take with him as many as he can.

Jesus promised that when the Holy Spirit came, He would guide us into all truth. He would not speak on His own initiative, but would teach only that which comes from the Father. Believing that truth would set us free. Jesus said, "He will glorify me because it is from me that he will receive what he will make known to you" (John 16:14). The Holy Spirit bears witness with our spirit that we are children of God (see Romans 8:16). We have become partakers of the divine nature (see 2 Peter 1:4). This is the great work of the Holy Spirit: to glorify the work of Jesus and make all this known to us in our inner person.

In the Bible, the word "mystery" means "that which has not been previously revealed." Paul tells us, "I have become [the Church's] servant by the commission God gave me to present to you the word of God in its fullness—the mystery that has been kept hidden for ages and generations, but is now disclosed to the Lord's people. To them God has chosen to make known among the Gentiles the glorious riches of this mystery, which is Christ in you, the hope of glory" (Colossians 1:25–27).

This is why we rejoice: our souls are in union with God. We are alive in Christ. We must learn to begin every day by acknowledging that the very presence of God is within us. Then we need to practice His presence throughout the day.

How can our Christian walk be distorted if we pursue power? How can it be distorted if we seek spiritual gifts for our own glorification?

_____

_____

_____

_____

Why did Jesus tell His disciples that it was better if He was *not* physically present with them?

_____

_____

_____

What is the greatest sin? How does the Holy Spirit work to make Christ known?

_____

_____

_____

_____

How can you discipline yourself to begin each day with God and practice His presence throughout the day?

_____

_____

_____

Why is it to your advantage to learn to live a spiritually disciplined life?

_____

_____

_____

The Lord sent the Paraclete because, since human weakness could not perceive everything at once, it might gradually be directed and regulated and brought to perfection of discipline by the Lord's vicar, the Holy Spirit. . . . And so, He declared the work of the Spirit. This, then, is the Paraclete's guiding office; the direction of discipline, the revelation of the Scriptures, the reforming of the intellect and the progress in us toward "better things."

Tertullian (AD 160–220)

5

Spiritual Wisdom
1 Corinthians 2:6–16

Key Point

When we choose to believe what God says is true, the Holy Spirit renews our minds and we begin to understand and see more clearly.

Key Verse

Without faith it is impossible to please God, because anyone who comes to him must believe that he exists and that he rewards those who earnestly seek him.

Hebrews 11:6

The Holy Spirit leads us into all truth, enables us to discern good from evil, and empowers us to live righteous lives. How He does this is difficult for the finite mind to comprehend, but Paul offers some explanation in 1 Corinthians 2:6–16.

First, the natural person cannot understand spiritual truth. The combined wisdom of the rulers of this world could never discern the wisdom of God. Had they been able to do so, they would not have crucified Christ. God's wisdom was hidden in the past but is now being revealed in the ultimate revelation of Christ. "No eye has seen, no ear has heard, and no mind has imagined what God has prepared for those who love him" (verse 9 NLT). It is humanly impossible to understand the wisdom of God through our natural channels of perception and our limited ability to reason, but "these are the things God has revealed to us by his Spirit" (verse 10).

Second, the Holy Spirit knows all things and is capable of revealing the nature of God and His will. "The Spirit searches all things, even the deep things of God" (verse 10). Third, as believers we have not received the spirit of this world, but we have received the Spirit who is from God. The Spirit makes known to us the things freely given by God. Fourth, we have the mind of Christ, because the very presence of God is within us. Fifth, the Holy Spirit takes words (*logos*) that are not taught by human wisdom but by the Spirit and combines (brings together, compares, or explains) them. What is actually being combined or compared is not clear—the original language literally reads "spirituals with spirituals." That phrase is translated in the New International Version as "words taught by the Spirit, explaining spiritual realities with Spirit-taught words" (verse 13).

We are transformed by the renewing of our minds (see Romans 12:2), and we are "to be made new in the attitude [literally, the spirit]" of our minds (Ephesians 4:23). The Holy Spirit discloses to us the mind of Christ as we study God's Word and then enables our thoughts and renews our minds with the *logos*. The peace of Christ rules in our hearts as the words of Christ richly dwell within us (see Colossians 3:15–16). Finally, the peace of God guards our hearts and our minds (see Philippians 4:7).

We may not fully understand how God does this, but we don't have to fully comprehend it in order to believe that He does. Nobody can fully explain the virgin birth of Jesus, the mystery of the Incarnation, the Holy Trinity, and the miracle of our new birth, but liberated Christians believe these truths, and understanding follows. When we choose to believe what God says is true, the Holy Spirit renews our minds, and we begin to understand and see more clearly.

Those who refuse to believe God and His Word until they fully understand will never fully understand. Those who choose to trust God and live accordingly by faith are blessed and begin to understand more fully as they mature in Christ. The disciple Thomas saw the resurrected Jesus and believed, prompting Jesus to say, "Blessed are those who have not seen and yet have believed" (John 20:29).

In what ways does the Holy Spirit give us wisdom and enable us to understand spiritual truth?

_____

_____

_____

_____

What does combining "spirituals with spirituals" mean?

_____

_____

_____

How do we allow the peace of Christ to rule in our hearts and guard our minds?

_____

_____

_____

Why can't you figure out the mysteries of God on your own?

_____

_____

_____

Are you waiting to fully understand the mysteries of God before you choose to believe, or have you chosen to believe in God and allow the mysteries to become clearer as you mature in your faith? What is the difference?

_____

_____

_____

_____

God gave us a mind in order that we might learn and receive help from Him, not in order that the mind should be self-sufficient. Eyes are beautiful and useful, but if they choose to see without light, their beauty is useless and may even be harmful. Likewise, if my soul chooses to see without the Spirit, it becomes a danger to itself.

John Chrysostom (AD 347–407)

Divine Providence

The providence of God refers to His direction and care over all creation. It is asserted in such texts as "[God] upholds all things by the word of His power" (Hebrews 1:3 NASB) and "we know that in all things God works for the good of those who love him, who have been called according to his purpose" (Romans 8:28). The way God "works for the good of those who love him" is a mystery to us, because it is humanly inscrutable and known of only by faith. Although the Bible affirms divine providence, it offers no explanation of the matter. Scripture portrays this mystery through narrative events.

One such narrative is of Joseph in the book of Genesis. As you read the story, you intuitively know that all things are working together for good, but

32

you don't know how. Every time Joseph tells the truth, he seems to suffer setbacks. His brothers throw him in a well to die, but he is brought back out and put on a caravan to Egypt. He is promoted from slavery to a favored position in the house of an official, only to be falsely accused and thrown in prison. Then he is brought out of prison to interpret the dreams of the king, which leads the way for his family to be reunited in Egypt. Reflecting on all this Joseph concludes, speaking to his ill-intentioned brothers, "It was not you who sent me here, but God" (Genesis 45:8).

Sometimes the Bible uses a narrative to reveal the providential nature of a story, such as David's escape from Saul at the hill of Hakilah (see 1 Samuel 26). "They were all sleeping, because the LORD had put them into a deep sleep" (verse 12). In the context of Absalom's revolt, the narrator says, "The LORD had determined to frustrate the good advice of Ahithophel in order to bring disaster on Absalom" (2 Samuel 17:14).

How God works all things together for our good will remain a mystery to us, but it does not preclude the need for us to assume responsibility for our own attitudes and actions. Providence is not fatalism. Foreknowledge does not mean that all events are predetermined; they are just pre-known.

The opening question of the Heidelberg Catechism (1563) cuts to the heart of divine providence. It begins by asking, "What is your comfort in life and death?" Answer: "That I, with body and soul, both in life and death, am not my own, but belong to my faithful Savior Jesus Christ who . . . so preserves me that without the will of my Father in heaven not a hair can fall from my head: yea, that all things work together for my salvation."

Spiritual Gifts

"Father, where shall I work today?"
And my love flowed warm and free.
Then He pointed out a tiny spot,
And said, "Tend that for Me."
I answered quickly, "Oh no, not that.
Why, no one would ever see,
No matter how well my work was done,
Not that little place for me!"
And the word He spoke, it was not stern;
He answered me tenderly,
"Ah, little one, search that heart of thine,
Art thou working for them or Me?
Nazareth was a little place,
And so was Galilee."[1]

—Mead MacGuire

Daily Readings

1. Equipped to Serve	1 Corinthians 12:4–11
2. Motivational Gifts	1 Peter 4:7–11
3. Public Use of Gifts	1 Corinthians 14:1–40
4. Life Endowments	Matthew 25:14–30
5. Stewardship	1 Corinthians 4:1–5

1

Equipped to Serve

1 Corinthians 12:4–11

Key Point

The Holy Spirit manifests spiritual gifts in the Body of Christ for the edification of all.

Key Verse

Now you are the body of Christ, and each one of you is a part of it.

1 Corinthians 12:27

The Holy Spirit indwells every born-again believer, enabling each person to live the Christian life and conform to the image and likeness of God. However, the ministry of the Holy Spirit is not just for individual edification. The sanctifying process requires that the whole Body of Christ work together. The Holy Spirit is the agent who equips individual members to serve one another in three ways.

First, each member has at least one gift of grace by which he or she ministers to the Body of Christ (see 1 Corinthians 12:4). Second, the Holy Spirit enables individual members to offer different kinds of service to the Church (see verse 5). Third, the Holy Spirit provides different kinds of workings within the Church, manifesting spiritual power in operation (see verse 6).

Paul argues that there is unity in diversity. All these manifestations of the Spirit have a unity in source. The "same Spirit" (verse 4), "same Lord [Jesus]" (verse 5), and "the same God" works all of them in everyone (verse 6). There is also a unity of purpose. These gifts, services, and manifestations are not given for personal edification but so that believers may build up one another: "Now to each one the manifestation of the Spirit is given for the common good" (verse 7).

Paul lists a variety of ways that the Spirit may manifest Himself among the believers. "To one there is given through the Spirit a message of wisdom, to another a message of knowledge . . . to another faith . . . to another gifts of healing . . . to another miraculous powers, to another prophecy, to another distinguishing between spirits, to another speaking in different kinds of tongues, and to still another the interpretation of tongues. All these are the work of one and the same Spirit, and he distributes them to each one, just as he determines" (verses 8–11).

The Body of Christ is made up of many parts, and all are necessary. Some members may feel unwanted or unnecessary when other gifts or manifestations of the Spirit seem to take on a greater prominence, "but God has put the body together, giving greater honor to the parts that lacked it, so that there should be no division in the body, but that its parts should have equal concern for each other" (verses 24–25). As the Body of Christ, we should eagerly desire the greater gifts to be manifested among us for the edification of all (see verse 31). We should not desire a greater gift for ourselves in order that we may be exalted above the others. God gives as He chooses, and we should gladly accept what He gives us and use it to the glory of God. We will never be fulfilled if we try to become somebody we aren't or try to acquire a gift that others have.

Paul gives no instruction for determining our own gifts. We should seek the Giver, not the gift; focus on being the person God intended us to be; and through love serve one another. In the process, our giftedness will become evident to all. A spiritual gift is a means to an end, not an end in itself. Various manifestations of the Spirit will come and go, but faith, hope, and love remain—and the greatest of these is love (see 13:13).

What are the three ways in which the Holy Spirit equips believers in the Church?

Why are spiritual gifts given to the Body of Christ?

What are some of the ways in which the Holy Spirit manifests Himself among believers?

In what way has God gifted you to serve others?

Why is it so important to accept the way God has created and gifted you? Why is it futile to try being someone else and seek some other gift of the Spirit?

Paul is here attributing to the Holy Spirit what he earlier at-tributed to all three persons. Because they are of one nature and power, the Three do what the One does. There is only one God, whose grace is distributed to individuals as He wishes, not according to the merits of any particular person, but for the upbuilding of His church. All those things which the world wants to imitate but cannot, because it is carnal, may be seen in the church, which is the house of God, where they are granted by the gift and instruction of the Holy Spirit.

Ambrosiaster (written c. AD 366–384)

2

Motivational Gifts

1 Peter 4:7–11

Key Point

God's grace is manifested to others as we use the gift that God has bestowed on us to serve one another with the strength that He provides.

Key Verse

We have different gifts, according to the grace given to each of us.

Romans 12:6

In 1 Peter 4:7–9, Peter advises us to be clear minded and committed to loving one another as the return of the Lord becomes more imminent. Love covers a multitude of sins, but love is not blind. Godly Christians see the faults and limitations of others and accept them for who they are in Christ. They will not only love their friends but will also offer hospitality, which literally means the love of strangers. They will use their gifts to serve others.

Gift (*charisma*) stems from God's grace (*charis*). His grace is manifested to others as we use the gift that God has bestowed on us to serve one another with the strength that God provides. In 1 Peter 4:10–11, Peter divides the gifts into two groups: speaking and service. "If anyone speaks, they should do so as one who speaks the very words of God. If anyone serves, they should do so with the strength God provides, so that in all things God may be praised through Jesus Christ" (verse 11). In Romans 12:4–8, Paul gives us a more complete list. These gifts motivate us to serve the Body of Christ in the following ways.

First, through the gift of prophecy. The word "prophecy" literally means "to speak forth" the mind and counsel of God. It can mean to foretell (predict future events) or forthtell (speak God's truth boldly to people). The primary emphasis is on the proclamation of God's Word. People with this gift are motivated to help others live righteous lives without judging them.

Second, through the gift of serving. This gift enables people to help others. People with this gift are motivated to respond to the needs of others in a practical way.

Third, through the gift of encouragement or exhortation. People with this gift encourage others to live out their faith according to God's Word. They are motivated to communicate God's Word in such a way that people listen and want to respond.

Fourth, through the gift of teaching. People with this gift are concerned about the authority of Scripture and doctrinal accuracy. They are motivated to rightly divide the word of truth and correct doctrinal error.

Fifth, through the gift of giving. People with this gift contribute to the financial needs of others and to the mission of the Church. They are motivated to be good stewards of the financial resources necessary to complete the mission of the Church.

Sixth, through the gift of leadership or administration. People with this gift provide the leadership and organizational structure necessary for effective ministry. They are motivated to organize the efforts of the Church for maximum efficiency.

Seventh, through the gift of mercy. This gift causes those who have it to feel deeply the spiritual and emotional needs of others. They are motivated to relieve pain and suffering and to provide comfort through prayer and personal assistance.

Every one of the above motivational gifts is needed in the Body of Christ. The different emphasis of each gift provides for a balanced ministry. We serve the Body of Christ best through our own giftedness. However, regardless of how we are gifted, we all need to speak the truth in love; be good stewards of our time, talent, and treasure; and love and serve one another.

How does the way in which we use our gifts manifest God's grace to others?

_____

_____

_____

Why is it important that we know there is a diversity of gifts that causes people to be motivated differently? What is the danger of emphasizing one or two gifts at the expense of others, or failing to recognize and appreciate the contribution of those motivated differently?

_____

_____

_____

How can we maintain unity among believers with such a diversity of gifts?

_____

_____

_____

How do you think God has equipped you to serve others?

_____

_____

_____

If you are not sure how you are gifted, what should you be pursuing? Are you content to allow your giftedness to become evident as you mature? Explain.

_____

_____

_____

By using the example of the body, Paul teaches that it is impossible for any one of us to do everything on our own, for we are members of each other and need one another. For this reason we ought to behave toward one another with care, because we need each other's gifts.

Ambrosiaster (written c. AD 366–384)

No one has the capacity to receive all spiritual gifts, but the grace of the Spirit is given proportionately to the faith of each one.

Basil the Great (AD 330–379)

3

Public Use of Gifts
1 Corinthians 14:1–40

Key Point

Christian men and women are gifted and the Church is edified when both are living under God's established order and using their gifts to the glory of God.

Key Verse

So what shall I do? I will pray with my spirit, but I will also pray with my understanding; I will sing with my spirit, but I will also sing with my understanding.

1 Corinthians 14:15

In 1 Corinthians 14, Paul is addressing a problem that had arisen in Corinth concerning public worship and the use of the gifts, specifically prophecy and tongues. In earlier chapters, Paul had discussed how Christians should live out their freedom, which was qualified and regulated by love. Now, a self-indulgent spirit, which had debauched the principle of freedom in other areas, had found a similar expression in the use of gifts for public worship. Such selfishness had produced disunity and chaos in public worship.

Paul said that whatever is done in the Church must be for the edification of all. Gifts are given for the common good (see 1 Corinthians 12) and must be used in agreement with the principle of love (see 1 Corinthians 13). There was no problem with any of the people using the service gifts excessively. The primary concern was the gift of prophecy and the gift of tongues—specifically their use in public worship. In response, Paul offered some prudent guidelines.

First, whatever is communicated in public worship must be intelligible. It must be spoken in the common language or at least be interpreted in the common language. Prophecy is more desirable than tongues (unless someone has the gift of interpretation), because prophecy is spoken in a language that can be understood by all present (see 1 Corinthians 14:1–3).

Second, because the Corinthians were eager to have spiritual gifts, they should "try to excel in those that build up the church" (verse 12). These gifts would certainly include serving, mercy, giving, administration, exhortation, and teaching, as well as prophecy. It seems to be part of our fallen nature to desire gifts that appear more supernatural and more noticeable by others. However, the exercise of any gift is supernatural, and God always notices its proper use.

Third, tongues is a sign for unbelievers, and the gift of prophecy is for believers because it communicates truth to those who are open to receiving it (see verse 22). Based on Paul's statement in verses 18 and 19, some would argue for the private use of tongues for their own edification. However, even the private use of tongues without an interpretation is unintelligible. Therefore, the personal benefit is subjective—that is, a sense of God's presence that enhances a love relationship. When a prophetic message is heard, "the secrets of their hearts are laid bare" (verse 25), which leads to repentance and thus draws them closer to God.

Fourth, "God is not a God of disorder but of peace" (verse 33). Paul has previously indicated that women can pray and prophesy in public worship as long as they are under authority (see 11:5). In this chapter, Paul seems to be prohibiting them from speaking in Church. Some argue that a woman should be in submission at home and church and that this timeless order was established at creation. Others understand this instruction to be sensitive to current social practices. In that culture it was "disgraceful for a woman to speak in the church" (1 Corinthians 14:35), but they reason it may not be so in other cultures.

Regardless of our understanding on this issue, we should always be respectful and "everything should be done in a fitting and orderly way" (verse 40). Christian men and women are gifted and the Church is edified when both are living under God's established order and using their gifts to the glory of God.

What specific problem is Paul addressing in 1 Corinthians 14?

_____

_____

_____

Why do you think Paul stresses that praying and singing with our spirits should also include singing and praying with our minds—and "in regard to evil be infants, but in your thinking be adults" (14:20)?

_____

_____

_____

What guidelines did Paul establish for the public use of the gift of tongues and prophecy?

_____

_____

_____

How can you personally distinguish between a gift from God and a counterfeit?

_____

_____

_____

How can you find the balance between an excessive emphasis on spiritual gifts and prohibiting their use?

_____

_____

_____

Paul wants them to be mature intellectually so they will grasp accurately what is needed for the upbuilding of the church. In this way they will leave behind malice and errors, striving instead for the things which are conducive to the good of the brotherhood.

Ambrosiaster (written c. AD 366–384)

Paul does not forbid speaking in tongues, however much he may belittle the gift, but he insists that it be kept under control and used for the edification of the whole church.

John Chrysostom (AD 347–407)

4

Life Endowments
Matthew 25:14–30

Key Point

What is important is not how much ability or opportunity you have but how faithful you are to use what you have been entrusted with.

Key Verse

So then, each of us will give an account of ourselves to God.

Romans 14:12

We have all been given some capacity to invest in the kingdom of God, and we will all give an account for our stewardship. Jesus teaches this principle in Matthew 25:14–30. In this parable, a man was going on a journey and gave his servants talents to invest. To the first he gave five talents, to the second he gave two talents, and to the third he gave one talent. They would be rewarded according to their ability (see verses 14–15).

The first and second servants doubled their investment, but the servant who received one talent buried it in the ground. When the master returned, he praised the two servants who had wisely invested their talents and put them in charge of greater things. They also got to share in their master's happiness (see verses 19–23).

This is an important principle for those who wish to grow in grace and expand their ministry. When God finds us faithful in the little things, He puts us in charge of greater things. We get out of life what we invest in it.

The man who was given one talent only had excuses. He didn't invest his talent because he felt that his master was a hard man who reaped where he did not sow (see verses 24–25). He reasoned, *My master probably isn't coming back anyway.* His perception of his master was wrong, and his failure to invest what had been entrusted to him cost him dearly (see verse 30). The master said, "You knew that I reap where I did not sow and gather where I scattered no seed. Then you ought to have put my money in the bank, and on my arrival I would have received my money back with interest" (verses 26–27 NASB).

A one-talented Christian may think that his one talent is not important, but if it were not for the one-talented Christians in our world, not much would be accomplished. The servant's one talent in the parable could have increased to two and brought glory to God. The parable of the talents teaches us to be faithful with whatever gifts or talents God has given us. This is not to be confused with the parable of the pounds in Luke 19:11–27, where each servant was given an amount equal to three months' pay but received a different reward. In the parable of the talents, the servants received different amounts but the same reward. What is important is not how much ability or opportunity you have but how faithful you are to use what you have been entrusted with.

There are two types of people who will never realize their potential: those who won't do what they are told and those who won't do anything unless they are told. You may not have any outstanding gifts or talents, but what you have you can put to good use. A timely word or act of kindness will pay future dividends. You may not lead many to Christ, but you may lead one who later leads many. In the end, God will judge you fairly according to your ability. "From everyone who has been given much, much will be demanded; and from the one who has been entrusted with much, much more will be asked" (Luke 12:48).

In the parable of the talents, why does the master praise his first two servants? What does this tell us about how God expects us to use His gifts and talents?

_____

_____

_____

Why didn't the servant with the one talent invest his gift? What was the result of his mismanagement of his master's money?

_____

_____

_____

What two types of people will never reach their potential? What limits them?

_____

_____

_____

Why is it so important to recognize what you have been entrusted with and then use it to the glory of God?

_____

_____

_____

Can you expect to be entrusted with bigger things if you have not shown yourself to be faithful in little things? Why or why not?

_____

_____

_____

But the third servant was unwilling to work with his talent. He returned to his master with words of excuse: "Master, I knew that you are a hard man, reaping where you have not sown, gathering where you have not scattered; being afraid, I went away and hid your talent in the earth. Here it is; see, you have what is yours." The useless servant called his master hard, and yet neglected to serve him for profit. He said that he was afraid to invest the talent for interest, when he should have been afraid only of bringing it back to his master without interest. For many people in the church resemble that servant. They are afraid to attempt a better way of life but not of resting in idleness. When they advert to the fact that they are sinners, the prospect of grasping the ways of holiness alarms them, but they feel no fear of remaining in their wickedness.

Gregory the Great (AD 540–604)

5

Stewardship

1 Corinthians 4:1–5

Key Point

We have been entrusted with the use of our lives and all that we possess, and someday we will give an account for how well we have managed the estate.

Key Verses

So we make it our goal to please him, whether we are at home in the body or away from it. For we must all appear before the judgment seat of Christ, so that each of us may receive what is due us for the things done while in the body, whether good or bad.

2 Corinthians 5:9–10

New life in Christ comes with an entitlement. "All things are yours . . . the world or life or death or the present or the future—all are yours, and you are of Christ, and Christ is of God" (1 Corinthians 3:21–23). We have all things because we are united to Christ and Christ with God the Father. However, we don't have ownership. We belong to God, and everything we possess belongs to Him. We are stewards of the

53

mysteries of God—the truth that has been revealed in the gospel of our Lord Jesus Christ.

A steward is someone who manages a household or estate. "Now it is required that those who have been given a trust must prove faithful" (4:2). We have been entrusted with the use of our lives and all that we possess, and someday we will give an account for how well we have managed the estate. There is no portion of our time that is ours while the rest is God's. There is no portion of our money that is ours while the rest is God's. It *all* belongs to Him. He made it all and simply entrusted it to us for His service. It doesn't matter what others think of our stewardship, or even what we think of ourselves. We can have a clear conscience, but that doesn't make us innocent. It is the Lord who judges us.

Jesus once told a parable about a rich fool. The man produced such a good crop that he had to tear down his barns and build bigger ones. Thinking that he had stored up enough to last for many years, he decided to take it easy—to eat, drink, and be merry. "But God said to him, 'You fool! This very night your life will be demanded from you. Then who will get what you have prepared for yourself?' This is how it will be with whoever stores up things for themselves but is not rich toward God" (Luke 12:20–21).

On another occasion, a rich young man asked Jesus how he could have eternal life. Jesus told him to keep the commandments, to which the rich man said he already did. Then Jesus said, "If you want to be perfect, go, sell your possessions and give to the poor, and you will have treasure in heaven. Then come, follow me" (Matthew 19:21). When the young man heard this, he walked away sad, because he had great wealth. Jesus showed the rich young man that his righteousness was self-righteousness and that his security was in his possessions, not in his eternal relationship with God.

"You may say to yourself, 'My power and the strength of my hands have produced this wealth for me.' But remember the LORD your God, for it is he who gives you the ability to produce wealth" (Deuteronomy 8:17–18). We are not called to be stewards of just the results of our labor but also the labor itself. Kingdom stewardship is like the Stradivari Society, which entrusts superb violins into the hands of the artists who make great music. We have enough time to do God's will. We have enough talent to fulfill our purpose. We have enough treasure to be satisfied. Those who think they don't have enough time, talent, or treasure have crowded God out of the center of their lives.

What is a steward? What does it mean to be a good steward?

What is the difference between ownership, entitlement, and entrustment?

What lessons can we draw from the parable of the rich fool?

How did the Lord reveal the false security and self-righteousness of the rich young ruler? What personal application can you take away from this teaching?

What is more precious to you—your time, your talent, your treasure, your life in Christ, or what matters for eternity? Explain.

_____

_____

_____

_____

A steward's duty is to administer well the things that have been entrusted to him. The things of the master's are not the stewards but the reverse—what is his really belongs to his master.

John Chrysostom (AD 347–407)

Wholistic Health

A woman named Nancy is fifty years old and exhibits many maladaptive psychological, physical, and spiritual symptoms. She feels lethargic about life, struggles with interpersonal relationships at home, and doesn't seem to connect at church. So she makes an appointment to see her doctor, who discovers that her blood sugar levels are high. In spite of the fact that Nancy is at least fifty pounds overweight, the doctor doesn't question her about her eating habits or lack of exercise. Her spiritual condition isn't considered as an option for treatment, so the doctor gives Nancy a written prescription for an oral diabetes medication to treat her prediabetic symptoms.

Nancy dutifully takes her medication and makes an appointment to see her pastor. He listens patiently about her struggle with depression and family problems. He asks about her prayer and devotional life, which are virtually nonexistent. He suggests that she spend more time with God on a daily basis and recommends a good book to partially replace her television "addiction." Meanwhile, she continues her same eating habits and tries to improve her spiritual disciplines.

The medication for her prediabetic condition gives her chronic indigestion, so she starts taking an H2 blocker like Tagamet, which reduces her digestive symptoms. However, now her stomach acid—which was low to begin with—is practically nonexistent. Consequently, she is not digesting food as well, which reduces her nutritional input. The medication also puts more stress on her kidneys, and because her estrogen level is low, she contracts a urinary tract infection. Nancy's doctor puts her on antibiotics for the condition, but that lowers her immune system and kills all the beneficial bacteria in her colon. The result is a bad case of the flu, which she can't seem to overcome, and she has constant discomfort from a colon imbalance.

Nancy soon starts taking antihistamines for a sinus infection, and her doctor recommends a hysterectomy to solve her urinary tract problem. The advice seems logical, so Nancy has the surgery and starts taking synthetic hormones, which make her feel depressed. She sees a psychiatrist, who writes out a prescription for Prozac to treat her depression. Nancy is now taking a diabetic medicine, an H2 blocker, antihistamines, synthetic hormones, and Prozac. She's exhausted all the time, mentally flaky, emotionally withdrawn, and waiting for the next health problem to hit.

Let's start over again. Instead of seeing her doctor, Nancy decides to confide with an encourager at church, who asks about her past and her present lifestyle. The encourager senses that Nancy has some unresolved personal and spiritual issues and invites her to attend a small group that is going to start a VICTORY SERIES study. Nancy's first inclination is to decline the offer, because another night out sounds like too much work for someone as exhausted as her. However, her friend reminds her that it would be good for her to get away from family responsibilities once a week and to do something for herself for a change.

Reluctantly, Nancy agrees to come to the Bible study. Her friend recognizes that she needs a lifestyle change and invites Nancy to come with her to the YMCA and start an exercise program that isn't too extreme. Nancy meets a new friend at the Bible study, who shares how she lost several pounds just by eating smarter. The two agree to meet and discuss proper nutrition.

Several months later, Nancy has found her freedom in Christ and has discovered what it means to be a child of God. Because of the encouragement of her friend she has stuck it out at the YMCA, and her energy level has increased significantly, due partly to her new eating habits. She has lost twenty pounds, and her blood sugar level is normal. She has also made some new friends at the YMCA and at the small group Bible study.

Growing Through Committed Relationships

On one side lay the hills—God's hills—green and verdant, quilted with trees, bordered by a brook. On the other lay the road—man's road—littered with cans and trash, weedy and winding, guarded by Joe's Beanery signs. Side by side they stood—a contrast—between God's creation of order, of beauty, of purpose, and man's works—unkempt, disfigured, and so outdated.

The house was carefully placed—the swing, the rockers, the windows, all took aim, alas, upon the road. It seemed to me—a shame, a mistake, almost a crime—to live in the hills and look at the road. Our generation—strangely afflicted, inwardly suffering from a disease that shows itself—in shriveled souls, in shallow thoughts, in spiritual myopia. Maybe this is the proper diagnosis—too many lives face the road, too few "look to the hills."

The hills—hills that can put us in perspective, hills that should inspire us to pray: "Oh Lord, make us serene like the hills, clear like the sky, pure like the clouds, upright like the trees, warm like the sunshine, refreshing like the rain, bubbling like the stream. O Thou Who makest all things—and maketh them beautiful—make us beautiful too."[1]

—Bob Benson, *Laughter in the Walls*

Daily Readings

1. The Importance of Community	Titus 2:1–15
2. Marriage, a Covenant Relationship	Malachi 2:10–16
3. Sexuality in the End Times	1 Corinthians 7:1–40
4. Training Up a Child	Ephesians 6:1–9
5. Disciplining Children	Malachi 4:1–6

1

The Importance of *~~Community~~* SOCIAL SOCIETY

Titus 2:1–15

Key Point

Godly character is forged in the crucible of committed relationships.

Key Verses

Therefore, as God's chosen people, holy and dearly loved, clothe yourselves with compassion, kindness, humility, gentleness and patience. Bear with each other and forgive one another if any of you has a grievance against someone.

Colossians 3:12–13

The sanctifying process is primarily worked out in our lives through committed relationships. There are two reasons for this. First, people can put on a public face and give others a false perception of who they are, but they can't consistently do that at home. Their spouses and children will see right through them.

Hypocrite

61

Second, marriage and family relationships (and, in Paul's letter, the slave-master relationship) were considered lifetime commitments. Rather than run away from the pressures of living together, we are supposed to stay committed to the relationship and grow up. Where better to learn to love one another, accept one another, forgive one another, and bear with one another than in the crucible of committed relationships? Notice that in Titus 2, Paul begins with an appeal for sound doctrine and ends with an appeal to godliness (see verses 1, 12–14). Within that context, he discusses the family and social relationships, just as he does in Ephesians and Colossians.

It is critically important to distinguish between who we are in Christ and our role responsibilities in life. When Paul led Onesimus, a runaway slave, to Christ, he sent him back to his earthly master. Paul appealed to Philemon to receive Onesimus as a brother in Christ (Philemon verses 10–11). During the time of Christ, a slave was more like a lifetime employee, and he or she often lived better than the self-employed (who were quite poor). In the case of Onesimus, being a slave was his social role; but he was first and foremost a child of God. This distinction can be clearly seen in Colossians 3:11, 22. In verse 11, Paul says in Christ there is neither slave or free, and then in verse 22 he talks about the role responsibility of slaves.

The same truth holds for husbands and wives. Husbands are to respect their wives as heirs with them of the gracious gift of life (see 1 Peter 3:7). In other words, Christian wives are children of God and equal in status with their Christian husbands. However, they don't have the same calling in life. In Titus 2, Paul gives specific instructions for older men, older women, younger women, young men, and slaves. He concludes by admonishing all to live godly lives.

In a general sense, Paul's epistles are divided into halves. The first half of each epistle is often considered theological, while the second half is considered practical. The tendency is to skip the first half and look to the second half for practical instruction on daily living. The result is a subtle form of Christian behaviorism: "You shouldn't do that; you should do this. That isn't the best way to do it; here is a better way."

Committed Christians will try the best they can to follow these rules, but they will often fail or burn out trying. Why doesn't it work for them, even though the behavioral objective is biblical? Because they have not first been established in Christ. If we can get believers to fully embrace the first half of Paul's epistles, they will be firmly rooted in Christ, and then they will be able to supernaturally live according to the second half. The goal is not to act like Christians, but to be children of God who live out their calling in life.

Why does God work primarily through committed relationships to forge our character?

_____

_____

_____

What will happen if we keep running away from committed relationships? Do you think God gives up on us, or does He keep the pressure on us until we finally learn to love one another?

_____

_____

_____

"There is neither . . . male and female, for you are all one in Christ Jesus" (Galatians 3:28). Why is it important to draw the distinction between who we are in Christ and our roles or calling in life (husbands and wives)?

_____

_____

_____

How should you perceive those with whom you live and work? How does that confront your character and living conditions?

_____

_____

_____

What relationship do you have (or have you had) that you would like to avoid or run away from that is pressuring you to deal with some unresolved issues in your own life? What is keeping you from doing the right thing?

_____

_____

_____

Nothing is wiser than the person who lives virtuously. . . . He gives what he owns, he is compassionate, he is loving to all. He has understood well that he shares a common human nature with others. He has thought through how to use his wealth wisely. He realizes the position of wealth makes no one special. He knows that the bodies of his relatives are more valuable than his wealth. The one who despises [personal] glory is wholly wise, for he understands human affairs. This is genuine philosophy, the knowledge of things divine and human. So then he comprehends what things are divine and what things are human. From the one he keeps himself, and to the other he devotes his labors. And he also knows how to thank God in all things. He considers the present life as nothing; therefore he is neither delighted with prosperity nor grieved with the opposite condition.

John Chrysostom (AD 347–407)

2

Marriage, a Covenant Relationship

Malachi 2:10–16

Key Point

Marriage is a covenant relationship between a man and a woman that is intended to reflect the covenant relationship that Christ has with the Church.

Key Verses

For this reason a man will leave his father and mother and be united to his wife, and the two will become one flesh. . . . They are no longer two, but one.

Matthew 19:5–6

The Lord wasn't pleased with the false worship of His covenant people. He explained why to the prophet Malachi: "You say, 'For what reason?' Because the LORD has been a witness between you and the wife of your youth, against whom you have dealt treacherously, though she is your companion and your wife by covenant. But not one has done so who has a remnant of the Spirit. And what did that one do while he was seeking a godly offspring? Take heed then to your spirit, and let no one deal treacherously against the wife of your youth. 'For I hate divorce,' says the Lord, the God of Israel" (2:14–16 NASB).

Divorcees hate divorce as well. Neither spouse feels good when he or she fails to keep the marriage commitments. Marriage is like gluing two pieces of paper together. Any attempt to separate them leaves both sheets damaged. Each spouse is left wounded—and the children of divorce will suffer as well. This is why God established marriage as a lifetime covenant. Unless abuse and infidelity are involved, the permanence of marriage protects the spouses and creates a healthy and stable environment in which to raise children. God is seeking godly offspring that come from a marriage between a man and woman who honor Him. Society can be no healthier than its marriages.

There are only two covenant relationships in this present age, and both are based on God's Word and rooted in His character. The first and foremost is our New Covenant relationship with God. The second is the marriage between a man and a woman. All other meaningful relationships are contractual or mutually convenient. Two people can have a covenant relationship with God and consequently have fellowship or spiritual kinship one with the other. However, they don't have a covenant relationship with each other unless they are married. While contractual relationships protect all parties in case one should default, marriage is not a contract that permits one spouse to leave when the other doesn't fulfill his or her expectations.

A covenant is a promise to fulfill regardless of the other person involved and is made to last regardless of circumstances. The wedding vows are a covenant commitment to stay faithful as a husband or wife, for better or for worse, for richer or for poorer, in sickness and in health, until death separates the two. Commitment is what makes a marriage relationship unique. Love, understanding, and forgiveness are what make it good. Romance makes it pleasurable. In marriage, the two become one in Christ, and together they help each other become more like Jesus.

In Matthew 19:3–12, Jesus admonished the Pharisees who had lost their commitment to stay married. They didn't want to commit adultery, because that was a capital offense under the law, so they were divorcing their wives for any little reason (see also Matthew 5:31–32). They were actually proliferating adultery, because they had no biblical grounds for divorce. Jesus said, "Moses permitted you to divorce your wives because your hearts were hard. But it was not this way from the beginning. I tell you that anyone who divorces his wife, except for sexual immorality, and marries another woman commits adultery" (Matthew 19:8–9).

According to Malachi 2:14–16, why was the Lord not pleased with His people? How did God describe His covenant with them?

_____

_____

_____

_____

Why did God establish marriage as a lifetime commitment?

_____

_____

_____

How does a covenant differ from a contract?

_____

_____

_____

How has the marriage or marriages of your parents affected you?

_____

_____

_____

How committed are you to your wedding vows (now or future), and to the sanctity of marriage?

_____

_____

_____

The union of Christ and the church is holy. So is the proper union of husband and wife holy. Just as a congregation of heretics, however, cannot be called the church of Christ and cannot have Christ as their head, so it is that a union between husband and wife cannot be truly called holy if there is a disregard for the way of life taught by Christ.

Jerome (AD 347–420)

3

Sexuality in the End Times
1 Corinthians 7:1–40

Key Point

Our relationship with God takes precedence over all matters of marriage.

Key Verse

Submit to one another out of reverence for Christ.

Ephesians 5:21

The background for Paul's teaching on marriage and sexuality was his belief that the present form of the world was passing away, that the second coming of Christ was near, and that life would be stressful. Paul's counsel is amazingly relevant for this contemporary world, whether you are single, betrothed, married to a believer, married to an unbeliever, or in a difficult marriage, divorced, or widowed. Paul's main concern, no matter what our matrimonial state, was to reinforce our devotion to the Lord (see 1 Corinthians 7:35). To that end, Paul urges single people never to put their desire for marriage higher than their desire to serve God (see verse 26) and to view their singleness as a gift and perhaps a lifelong calling from God (see verse 7).

Paul realizes that Christians are going to be attracted to people of the opposite sex and tempted into immorality (verses 1–2), so he places boundaries on available partners and on behavior (see verse 34). First, believers should not marry unbelievers (see 2 Corinthians 6:14–16), because the righteous have nothing in common with the unrighteous. They would be unequally yoked with different values, standards, and direction in life. Second, for the sake of Christian ministry, it is good for a man not to marry. However, because there is so much immorality, each man should have his own wife, and each woman her own husband (see 7:1–2).

Those already married are not to withhold themselves from each other sexually. Their bodies not only belong to themselves but also to each other for mutual sexual fulfillment. However, no spouse can satisfy the other spouse's lust. That can only be resolved in their relationship with God. Neither spouse has the right to violate the other person's conscience or defile him or her physically in any way, because that person's body is the temple of God (see 1 Corinthians 6:19). Sexual intimacy and fulfillment in marriage can only happen in the context of mutually shared love and trust.

Paul advises Christian couples not to separate, but if they do, to remain unmarried and work toward reconciliation. There are times when a relationship can be so strained that separation may be necessary for the good of the family. Ideally, the couple should stay together and work it out. However, if one spouse becomes physically or mentally abusive, it may be advisable to separate, but not divorce unless there are scriptural grounds for such action. Scripture teaches that wives and children should be submissive, but Scripture also teaches that governing authorities have the right to punish wrongdoers (see Romans 13:4). Those in authority have the responsibility to provide and protect. In cases of abuse, the state has the right to intervene, protect battered wives and abused children, and prosecute the offenders.

There are only two grounds for divorce and remarriage. The first is abandonment by an unbelieving spouse. Should a couple be unequally yoked, the believer must stay committed to the marriage for the purpose of his or her spouse's salvation. The unbeliever can leave, and if he or she does, the believer is not bound to the marriage (see 1 Corinthians 7:15). The second is adultery and, some would argue, sexual perversion. Under the Law, the adulterer would have been stoned to death, so obviously the remaining spouse would be free to remarry. Under grace, forgiveness and reconciliation should be attempted, but if not successful, the faithful spouse has the right to divorce and remarry.

What is Paul's main concern for believers as they consider marriage in the future or their present circumstances? Why should that take precedence in every situation?

_____

_____

_____

Why is the marriage between believers and unbelievers prohibited?

_____

_____

_____

Under what conditions might it be necessary for a couple to separate? What should always be the goal of any separation?

_____

_____

_____

What part of Paul's teaching do you struggle with the most? How has it kept you on the right path?

_____

_____

_____

What concerns you the most about the direction our culture is headed concerning marriage and family?

_____

_____

_____

Have you noted the measure of obedience? Pay attention to love's high standard. If you take the premise that your wife should submit to you, as the church submits to Christ, then you should also take the same kind of careful, sacrificial thought for her that Christ takes for the church. Even if you must offer your own life for her, you must not refuse. Even if you undergo countless struggles on her behalf and have all kinds of things to endure and suffer, you must not refuse. Even if you suffer all this, you have still not done as much as Christ has for the church. For you are already married when you act this way, whereas Christ is acting for one who has rejected and hated Him. So just as He, when she was rejecting, hating, spurning and nagging Him, brought her to trust Him by His great solicitude, not by threatening, lording it over her, or intimidating her or anything like that, so you must also act toward your wife. Even if you see her looking down on you, nagging and despising you, you will be able to win her over with your great love and affection for her.

John Chrysostom (AD 347–407)

The Rise and Fall of Great Civilizations

For his 1934 work *Sex and Culture*, British anthropologist J. D. Unwin studied eighty societies, analyzing their cultural beliefs and practices, especially

72

as they related to sex and marriage. He examined the "cultural condition" of these societies, by which he meant the developmental status and energy they manifested. Was the culture growing—demonstrating what he called "expansive energy"? Then, later in its history, was it improving what it had built—what he called "productive energy"?

Unwin said that whether or not a society had moved from an uncivilized state to a civilized state, and whether it was manifesting creative energy, was a direct product of how sexually permissive the culture was. He defined this by identifying various degrees of "sexual opportunity." The more sexual opportunity a society's people had—that is, the fewer restraints placed upon sexual habits—the less energetic it would be.

"In the records of history," Unwin said, "indeed, there is no example of a society displaying great energy for any appreciable period unless it has been absolutely monogamous. Moreover, I do not know of a case in which an absolutely monogamous society has failed to display great energy."[1]

Likewise, in his 1956 work *The American Sex Revolution*, Pitirim A. Sorokin, who founded the sociology department at Harvard University, wrote,

> Since a disorderly sexual life tends to undermine the physical and mental health, the morality, and the creativity of its devotees, it has a similar effect upon a society that is composed largely of profligates (grossly indulgent). And the greater the number of profligates, and the more debauched their behavior, the graver are the consequences for the whole society. And if sexual anarchists compose any considerable proportion of its membership, they eventually destroy the society itself.[2]

Sorokin stated that in the decline of ancient Egypt, "Sexual anarchy assumed extreme forms and spread through a large part of the population. Side by side with an increase of sexual perversions, a shameless sexual promiscuity also greatly increased." He also cited a historian who said about this period of Egyptian decline,

> Homosexual love entered the mores of the population. The contemporary authors seem to sadistically enjoy the enumeration of a variety of turpitudes and sexual perversions. . . . They describe all the aberrations of morbid

eroticism with the impudent serenity of the casuist: rape, unnatural sexual relations, and sodomy.[3]

Unwin stated that in ancient Athens during the fifth century,

The old customs had disappeared, the sexual opportunity of both sexes being extended. There was no compulsory continence; sexual desires could be satisfied in a direct manner. Divorce became easy and common; homosexual sex between men and boys appeared; the men possessed mistresses as well as wives; the women broke bounds, consoling themselves with both wine and clandestine love affairs. The energy of the Athenians declined. Three generations later, the once vigorous city, torn by dissension, was subject to a foreign master.[4]

Sorokin stated that during the decline of the Roman republic,

The growth of sexual anarchy, divorces, desertions and orgies; of emancipation and 'masculinization' of women and effemination of men, together with radical changes in marriage and family laws, which largely dissolved their sacredness and inviolability, and an attendant decrease of birth rate, proceeded hand in hand with a growth of irreligiosity and of vulgar sensualist ethics and frame of mind.[5]

The one lesson that we learn from history is that we never seem to learn from history. We know this because history keeps repeating itself! Since the sexual revolution of the 1960s, the United States continues to decline in sexual morality. Session four will address this critical issue from God's perspective. There is always hope. "If my people, who are called by my name, will humble themselves and pray and seek my face and turn from their wicked ways, then will I hear from heaven, and I will forgive their sin and will heal their land" (2 Chronicles 7:14).

4

Training Up a Child
Ephesians 6:1–9

Key Point

Parents should be students of their children and help them become what God intended them to be.

Key Verse

Train up a child in the way he should go, and when he is old he will not depart from it.

Proverbs 22:6 NKJV

All the nurture in the world cannot make a rose out of a tulip. Parents have to train up children in the way they should go, not the way the parents want them to go. Consequently, parents need to be students of their own children and assist them in being what God has intended them to be. To accomplish this, parents have to adopt the right parenting style. The following diagram depicts four different styles:

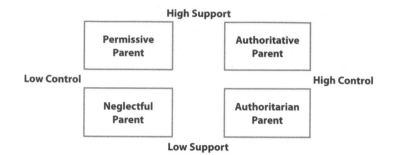

The two most powerful influences in parenting are *control* and *support*. Control is the parent's ability to manage a child's behavior, while support is the ability to make a child feel loved. By definition, *authoritative* parents have the ability to make their children feel loved and the ability to manage their behavior. *Permissive* parents love their children but neglect to manage their behavior. *Neglectful* parents do neither. *Authoritarian* parents try to control their children's behavior but neglect loving support.

Research has shown that children of authoritative parents have the highest sense of worth, conform most easily to authority, are most likely to accept their parents' religion, and are least likely to rebel against societal norms. Permissive parents produce children who rank second in all four categories just mentioned. Children of neglectful parents rank third, while children of authoritarian parents rank last.

Obviously, it is more important that you help your children feel loved than it is to control their behavior. You may not be able to control your children's behavior, but you can always love them because your ability to love is not dependent on the children. Research reinforces what Paul wrote: "Fathers, do not exasperate your children; instead, bring them up in the training and instruction of the Lord" (Ephesians 6:4).

Children ask two questions: "Do you love me?" and "Can I get my own way?" Permissive parents answer yes to both questions and potentially spoil the child. Neglectful parents allow their children to have their own way. The child who doesn't feel loved and gets his or her own way has the greatest potential to become a juvenile delinquent. Authoritarian parents answer no to both questions, which leads to rebellion.

Tragically, many parents resort to authoritarianism when problems surface in the home, which produces the worst fruit. The overly controlled and under-loved child is either riddled with guilt and shame or rebels against authority. Authoritative parents set boundaries and maintain discipline while demonstrating genuine love. They have the best chance of producing a well-adjusted child.

Why do parents need to be students of their children?

Why does loving a child take precedence over controlling a child?

Why do so many parents resort to controlling their children? Do they do so for their benefit or for the child's benefit? Explain.

Which parenting style did your father adopt? How has that impacted you?

Which parenting style did you mother adopt? How has that impacted you? Which of your parents are you most like?

_____

_____

_____

Then he [Paul] explains the all-important thing about parenting; how children are to be brought to obedience. He traces the motive of obedience back to its source and fountain. He has already shown how the husband's behavior elicits the wife's obedience when he spoke primarily to the husband, advising him to draw her to him by the bonds of love. Similarly here also he shows how the parent's behavior elicits the children's obedience, saying, "Rear them in the instruction and discipline of the Lord." Do you see when the spiritual motives are present, the physical effects will follow along? Do you want your son to be obedient? Rear him from the onset in the teaching and discipline of the Lord. Never regard it as a small matter that he should be a diligent learner of Scriptures.

John Chrysostom (AD 347–407)

5

Disciplining Children

Malachi 4:1–6

Key Point

Discipline is a proof of your love.

Key Verse

No discipline seems pleasant at the time, but painful. Later on, however, it produces a harvest of righteousness and peace for those who have been trained by it.

Hebrews 12:11

The prophecy concerning Elijah in Malachi 4:5–6 was probably fulfilled by the coming of John the Baptist. He ministered "in the spirit and power of Elijah" (Luke 1:17) and prepared the way for Jesus, who brought new life. It is this new life in Christ that will turn the hearts of parents and children toward each other.

Parents play a role much like that of John the Baptist, who said, "He must become greater; I must become less" (John 3:30). Mothers and fathers play the dominant role in shaping the lives of their children when

79

their children's only identity and heritage is physical. It is the goal of all Christian parents to lead their children to Christ, but they need to do more. They must help their children realize that they are children of God and have an inheritance in Christ.

Proverbs 29:17 says, "Discipline your children, and they will give you peace; they will bring you the delights you desire." Discipline is a proof of your love, and it is meant to superintend future choices, while punishment is retroactive and too often administered out of revenge. There are many ways to discipline, but not every child responds the same way to the same discipline. For this reason, you must understand your children to know which of the following forms of discipline is appropriate for them. The hardest task for some is to remain consistent in their discipline.

Communication is the most common form of discipline. Parents should make a clear statement of their expectations and the consequences for disobedience. A rule should be definable, defensible, and enforceable. Verbal communication after disobedience is a powerful form of discipline. Even silence communicates volumes. When children know they have disappointed their parents, it can be more painful for them than a spanking.

Natural consequences that allow children to experience the effects of their disobedience and irresponsible behavior can be effective, especially for strong-willed children. Some children just have to learn the hard way. Rescuing children from their mistakes can seriously impede their growth. They need to understand the connection between cause and effect.

Logical consequences, such as assigning chores or restricting privileges that are connected to the sin or disobedience, can effectively teach children to be responsible.

Reinforcement, where parents catch their children doing something right and reward their good behavior, leads to behavior that is more likely to be repeated. If your children only get your attention when they are doing something wrong, you are not training them for righteousness. The results are the same as trying not to think bad thoughts when you should be choosing to think the truth.

Extinction is a way of ignoring attention-getting behaviors such as crying or throwing temper tantrums. If children just have their tantrum, they begin to realize it isn't working. The children are training the parent when it works. Wise parents don't honor such manipulative techniques by paying attention to them.

Spanking, according to the Bible, can be used to discipline negative behavior. Spanking should not be used for punishment but for the purpose of shaping future behavior—and it is probably most effective in the first two years of the child's life. Parents should never spank children to get even or vent their frustration. Spanking should always be done in love, using an instrument other than the parent's hand.

How does the new life we receive in Christ turn the hearts of parents and children toward one another?

_____

_____

_____

_____

What is the difference between discipline and punishment?

_____

_____

_____

Why is catching your children doing something right even more important than catching them doing something wrong?

_____

_____

_____

_____

If discipline is a proof of your love for your children, should you try to discipline them when you are angry and have lost control of yourself (that is, when you are responding according to the flesh)? Why or why not?

What should you do if you have punished your child in anger and frustration?

You are suffering, he says. For such is chastisement; such is its beginning. "For the moment all discipline seems painful rather than pleasant." He said well, "seems." Discipline, he means, is not grievous but "seems" so. "All discipline" means both human and spiritual. Do you see that he argues from common notions? "Seems painful," he says, so that it is not really so. For what sort of pain brings forth joy? So neither does pleasure bring forth despondency. Nevertheless, "Later it yields the peaceful fruits of righteousness to those who have been trained by it." Not "fruit" but "fruits," a great abundance.

John Chrysostom (AD 347–407)

Overcoming Sexual Bondage

Rick was riding a spiritual and emotional roller coaster. His convictions would drive him to break off relationships and return to the Lord. Then personal problems and depression would lead him back to the same old flesh patterns of sex and food. Rick explained his futile attempts to control his behavior:

> The "pimp" in my mind repeatedly promised me fulfillment if I would only prostitute myself one more time. But the lies never fulfilled their promises. Life for me was like pushing a car. When things were going all right, it required only a little effort. But every time I tried to push the car over the mountain of my sexual bondage, the car rolled back over me—leaving me desperate, hurt, and hopeless. I couldn't stop this cycle no matter how much I sought God. My sexual addiction ruled everything in my life. I hated it. I knew it was destroying me from the inside—but I kept heeding the pimp in my mind again and again.

Rick's godly mother encouraged him to attend a Living Free in Christ conference. During the first evening of the conference, he was harassed by sexual fantasies in his mind. However, he did hear one statement that gave him some hope: "If the Son sets you free, you will be free indeed" (John 8:36). Rick knew he wasn't free—that he was powerless to stop the fruitless search for fulfillment and satisfaction in sex, food, and work. Later, after the conference, he shared this testimony:

> I knew while driving to the meeting that something was going to happen. My heart felt like it was going to explode. There was a war raging within me. The pimp in my mind who had controlled my life for years didn't want me to go. But I was determined to experience freedom in Christ.
>
> I expected to receive a slap on the side of the head and an exorcistic prayer shouted at me. Then I would surely fall to the floor and flop around unconditionally until the effects of the prayer set me free. It didn't happen that way. Instead, I simply learned that I *could* be set free in Christ.
>
> As I went though the Steps to Freedom in Christ, I could hear the pimp's insistent lies in my mind. The inner battle was intense, but I was ready for the shackles to be broken. So I repented of my sin, renounced all the lies I had believed, renounced every sexual use of my body as an instrument of unrighteousness, and forgave all those who had offended me. As I did, peace began to roll in and drown out thirty-seven years' worth of lies. I sensed a holy silence in my mind. The pimp was gone and, praise God, I was free.

Rick's freedom was tested right away. The next day during the conference, he was bombarded by immoral thoughts. But he took those thoughts captive to the obedience of Christ and chose to believe the truth that he was a child of God, alive and free in Christ. That night he was tempted to pursue another destructive relationship. He called upon the Lord, and the "holy silence" returned. Rick has since experienced a genuine and growing relationship with his heavenly Father. He stopped watching the raunchy television programs and movies that played a large part in feeding his lustful habits. His newfound freedom in Christ resulted in a desire to study the Bible and pray, which before were tiresome religious duties to be performed.[1]

Daily Readings

1. The Downward Spiral of Obsession	2 Samuel 13:1–22
2. Foolish Thinking	Proverbs 7:6–27
3. The Entrapment of Sin	2 Chronicles 29:1–36
4. Sexual Bonding	1 Corinthians 6:9–20
5. Sin Dwelling in You	Romans 7:14–25

1

The Downward Spiral
of Obsession

2 Samuel 13:1–22

Key Point

The downward spiral of sexual obsession leads to bondage, sickness, and death.

Key Verse

Do not lust in your heart after her beauty or let her captivate you with her eyes.

Proverbs 6:25

What starts with an innocent attraction for a person of the opposite sex can become an infatuation that leads to mental obsession. In 2 Samuel 11, David saw that Bathsheba was beautiful, but he didn't look for God's way of escape. He stepped over a moral boundary when he sent someone to find out about her.

David's weakness may have contributed to his son Amnon's obsession with Tamar, "the beautiful sister of Absalom son of David" (2 Samuel 13:1).

Solomon warned in Proverbs 6:25–26, "Do not lust in your heart after her beauty or let her captivate you with her eyes. For a prostitute can be had for a loaf of bread, but another man's wife preys on your very life." Amnon played out his sexual fantasy for Tamar so many times in his mind that he became physically sick.

It is no sin to be tempted, and when we are tempted, God provides a way of escape (see 1 Corinthians 10:13). However, we miss that opportunity when we continue to entertain lustful thoughts in our mind. James says, "But each one is tempted when he is carried away and enticed by his own lust. Then when lust has conceived, it gives birth to sin; and when sin is accomplished, it brings forth death" (1:14–15 NASB). Amnon had carried on a sexual affair with Tamar for some time in his mind, and his obsessive thoughts screamed for expression. So Amnon and his friend Jonadab concocted a plan to get Tamar into Amnon's bed (see 2 Samuel 13:3–5).

Once a plan to fulfill the demands of lust is set in motion, it can seldom be stopped. Amnon had lost control, and where there is no self-control, all reason is gone. Amnon's sexual obsession had reduced him to a "loaf of bread"—powerless to stop the runaway train of his desires. Tamar tried to reason with Amnon, but he was "like one of the wicked fools in Israel" (verse 13). Amnon violated her with no regard for the damage it would do to either of them. "Then Amnon hated her with intense hatred. In fact, he hated her more than he had loved her" (verse 15).

People in bondage hate the sin that controls them. After consuming their fill, alcoholics throw the empty bottle against the wall in disgust, only to buy another when the cravings return. Lust cannot be satisfied. The more you feed it, the more it grows. In early development, one can be sexually stimulated by a sensual look or simple touch. The rush of a lustful thought or sexual encounter leads to a euphoric experience, but it doesn't last. A sense of guilt and shame follows, but inwardly there is the desire to have that euphoric experience again. Every repeated exposure leads to greater sexual degradation in order to reach that same euphoric experience. The downward spiral of guilt and shame leads to greater bondage, sickness, and death.

We see evidence of this everywhere in our world today. In the United States alone, there are nineteen million new infections of sexually transmitted diseases each year.[1] The porn industry generates roughly $14 billion in revenue annually.[2] In addition, 50 percent of those who stay in hotel rooms will purchase adult entertainment.[3]

In 2 Samuel 13:1–22, how did Amnon's attraction for Tamar turn into obsession?

_____

_____

_____

What damage did Amnon cause to himself and others by allowing his lust to consume him?

_____

_____

_____

Is immoral sex between consenting adults a private affair, or do such acts have larger social consequences? Explain.

_____

_____

_____

Since everyone is tempted, how can you learn to recognize the temptation and take that initial thought captive to the obedience of Christ?

_____

_____

_____

What will happen if you don't take that initial way of escape and allow your mind to be "carried away"?

_____

_____

_____

If we sin when we are drunk with pleasure, we do not notice it. But when it gives birth and reaches its goal, then all the pleasure is extinguished and the bitter core of our mind comes to the surface. . . . Therefore I beg you right from the start not to welcome any corrupt thought, for if we do so the seeds will grow inside us, and if we get to that stage, the sin inside us will come out in deeds and strike us dead by condemning us, in spite of all our confessions and tears. For there is nothing more destructive than sin.

John Chrysostom (AD 347–407)

2

Foolish Thinking

Proverbs 7:6–27

Key Point

Genuine righteousness is a matter of the heart, not the result of fruitless attempts in our own strength to behave according to external standards.

Key Verse

Since we live by the Spirit, let us keep in step with the Spirit.

Galatians 5:25

The simple young man in Proverbs 7 lacked judgment (see verse 7). He had no idea that his naïveté would cost him his life (see verses 22–23). The woman who seduced him was dressed like a prostitute, supposedly religious (see verse 14), and married (see verse 19). A wise man would have seen the danger and discerned immediately that her intentions were not good, but a simple person doesn't consider the consequences of sin. The fool wants only immediate gratification.

AIDS is one of the most devastating diseases in the modern age and is among the most incurable diseases in the world, but by far it is the most preventable. All one generally has to do is abstain from immoral sex and the use of illegal drugs. While AIDS can be transmitted through blood transfusions and occupational exposure (such as in a health care setting), the majority of cases are caused by sexual contact and injection drug use.[1] Millions of people are living with AIDS, and millions have died from it since it was first detected in 1981.[2] To throw away your life, career, marriage, and reputation for a few minutes of sexual pleasure is totally irrational.

Jesus tells us, "You have heard that it was said, 'You shall not commit adultery.' But I tell you that anyone who looks at a woman lustfully has already committed adultery with her in his heart. If your right eye causes you to stumble, gouge it out and throw it away. It is better for you to lose one part of your body than for your whole body to be thrown into hell. And if your right hand causes you to stumble, cut it off and throw it away" (Matthew 5:27–30). Jesus is graphically illustrating the seriousness of sexual sin. We should be willing to sacrifice whatever it takes to keep from paying a far greater cost for the inevitable consequences of adultery: disease and death.

However, our eyes and hands are not the culprits when we sin. Cutting off body parts will not solve the problem. Jesus explains that those who look lustfully at another person have *already* committed adultery in their hearts. The looking is the *evidence*, not the cause. In the Sermon on the Mount, He teaches that genuine righteousness is a matter of the heart, not the result of behavioral conformity to external laws. "For I tell you that unless your righteousness surpasses that of the Pharisees and the teachers of the law, you will certainly not enter the kingdom of heaven" (verse 20). The prevention of murder (see verses 21–26) and adultery (see verses 27–32) requires a transformation of our hearts and a renewing of our minds.

Salvation does not improve our old nature. Salvation makes us a new creation in Christ and a partaker of the divine nature (see 2 Peter 1:4). "Those who belong to Christ Jesus have crucified the flesh with its passions and desires" (Galatians 5:24). In Christ we have the potential not to sin because of what Christ has already accomplished for us, but we have to assume our responsibility. First, we must choose to believe the truth and repent of our sins. Second, we must live by the Spirit and not carry out the desires of the sinful nature (see Galatians 5:16). Third, we must renew our minds and "take captive every thought to make it obedient to Christ" (2 Corinthians 10:5).

How did the simple young man in Proverbs 7 show lack of judgment? What did his foolish thinking cost him?

_____

_____

_____

In Matthew 5:21–32, Jesus says that if you call your brother a name you are guilty of murder, and if you look at another woman in lust you are guilty of adultery. Is Jesus saying this to condemn us, or is He teaching us how to prevent murder and adultery? Explain.

_____

_____

_____

What is genuine righteousness?

_____

_____

_____

How can you prevent yourself from injuring others and committing sexual sins?

_____

_____

_____

Only you and God know how genuine your righteousness really is. How important is it to you that what others see is who you really are? How can you make that happen?

_____

_____

_____

For he did not simply say, "whoever shall desire," since it is possible for one to desire when sitting alone in the mountains. Rather, Jesus said, "Whoever looks with lust"; that is, one who thinks about another solely for the purpose of lusting, who, under no compulsion, allows the wild beast to intrude upon his thoughts when they are calm. This intrusion no longer comes from nature but from self-indulgence. . . . For when you look once, twice, or three times, you will perhaps have power to refrain; but if you make this your habitual practice, kindling the furnace within you, you will assuredly be overcome. Your human nature is no different from that of other people.

John Chrysostom (AD 347–407)

3

The Entrapment of Sin

2 Chronicles 29:1–36

Key Point

We allow sin to reign in our mortal bodies when we use them as instruments of unrighteousness.

Key Verse

What is the source of quarrels and conflicts among you? Is not the source your pleasures that wage war in your members?

James 4:1 NASB

The revival that occurred in Judah during Hezekiah's reign is a model of repentance for the Church and a foretaste of the gospel. The account in 2 Chronicles 29 tells us that Hezekiah did three things to enable this revival to happen. First, he consecrated the priests and cleaned out the Temple (see verses 15–16). As New Testament believers, we are priests and our bodies are temples of God. Second, Hezekiah ordered the sin offering. The sin offering was a blood offering only—the carcass of the sacrificed animal was disposed of outside the walls of the city. Jesus is our sin offering, and after shedding His blood, His body was entombed outside the walls of the city.

Third, Hezekiah ordered the burnt offering, which involved the sacrifice of the whole body of the animal. In this context, "burnt" literally means "that which ascends." When Hezekiah ordered this offering, the music in the Temple began (see verse 27). Under the New Covenant, we are the burnt offering: "Therefore, I urge you, brothers and sisters, in view of God's mercy, to offer your bodies as a living sacrifice, holy and pleasing to God—this is your true and proper worship" (Romans 12:1). It is not enough for us to know that our sins are forgiven. We must yield ourselves to God as *living* sacrifices, and then the music begins in our temples as He fills us with His Spirit. We will speak "to one another with psalms, hymns, and songs from the Spirit. Sing and make music from your heart to the Lord" (Ephesians 5:19).

Believers consider themselves to be alive in Christ and dead to sin. "Therefore do not let sin reign in your mortal body so that you obey its evil desires" (Romans 6:12). That is our responsibility, and the next verse tells us how—including one negative instruction and two positive instructions: "Do not offer any part of yourself to sin as an instrument of wickedness, but rather offer yourselves to God as those who have been brought from death to life; and offer every part of yourself to him as an instrument of righteousness" (verse 13). Personal revival and victory come when we clean out the temple through genuine repentance and choose to consecrate ourselves *and* our bodies to God as instruments of righteousness.

If we commit a sexual sin, we have used our bodies as instruments of unrighteousness, which allows sin to reign in our mortal bodies. Thank God our sins are forgiven in Christ, but the music won't begin in our temple until we fully repent. Confession is the first step in repentance, but that by itself will not resolve the entrapment of sin. We need to renounce every use of our bodies as instruments of unrighteousness and then submit our bodies to God as living sacrifices.

The process is complete when we have fully submitted to God *and* resisted the devil (see James 4:7). (The Steps to Freedom in Christ provide a comprehensive overview of the process of repentance.) If we have dealt with sin's entrapment and yielded our bodies to God as living sacrifices (see Romans 12:1), then the process of being transformed by the renewing of our minds becomes possible (see 12:2).

According to 2 Chronicles 29, what three things did King Hezekiah do that enabled revival to happen in Judah?

_____

_____

_____

_____

What does it mean to yield our lives to God as "living sacrifices"?

_____

_____

_____

How does sin "reign" (rule) in our mortal bodies?

_____

_____

_____

Why would it be difficult to win the battle for our minds without first dealing with sin's entrapment?

_____

_____

_____

How could you orchestrate your own revival by following Hezekiah's three-step plan?

_____

_____

_____

God's will is our sanctification, for bodies subject to sin are considered not to be alive but dead, since they have no hope of obtaining the promised eternal life. It is for this purpose that we are cleansed from our sins by God's gift, that henceforth we should lead a pure life and stir up the love of God in us, not making His work of grace of no effect. For the ancients killed sacrifices which were offered in order to signify that men were subjected to death because of sin. But now, since by the gift of God men have been purified and set free from the second death, they must offer a living sacrifice as a sign of eternal life. For now it is no longer the case that bodies are sacrificed for bodies, but instead of bodies it is the sins of the body which must be put to death.

Ambrosiaster (written c. AD 366–384)

4

Sexual Bonding
1 Corinthians 6:9–20

Key Point

Believers are one in spirit with the Lord and should not become one flesh with another through immoral sex.

Key Verse

Flee from sexual immorality. All other sins a person commits are outside the body, but whoever sins sexually, sins against their own body.

1 Corinthians 6:18

Some in the Corinthian church believed that the body was not important because it was transitory. Therefore, they thought that eating food and being promiscuous had no bearing on their spiritual life. Paul countered this belief by telling them ("The body, however, is not meant for sexual immorality but for the Lord, and the Lord for the body" (1 Corinthians 6:13). As believers, our bodies are temples of God and members of Christ Himself. We have been purchased by the blood of the Lamb, and our body, soul, and spirit belong to Him.

"Do you not know that your bodies are members of Christ himself? Shall I then take the members of Christ and unite them with a prostitute? Never! Do you not know that he who unites himself with a prostitute is one with her in body? For it is said, 'The two will become one flesh'" (1 Corinthians 6:15–17). Being "one with her in body" is an immoral bond. Paul explained that using our bodies as instruments of unrighteousness allows sin to reign in our mortal bodies (see Romans 6:12–14).

The entrapment of sexual sin is commonly manifested in three ways. First, promiscuous sex before marriage leads to a lack of sexual fulfillment after marriage. Second, a believer who is sexually united with an unbeliever becomes bonded in such a way that the Christian can't break away without genuine and complete repentance. Third, for many believers who have been violated sexually before marriage against their will (rape or incest), it undermines their ability to perform freely in marriage. Many women who have been sexually violated are left with the impression that sex is dirty, and they don't like to be touched, even by their spouses. Some pervert has violated their temple. The opposite effect is often the result for those who voluntarily had sex with family members before marriage. Many of these people can't be sexually satisfied and continuously seek sexual fulfillment with multiple partners.

Suppose a nice Christian young lady gets sexually involved with the wrong man. He treats her horribly, but she stays with him. Friends and family counsel her to leave him, but she refuses. Why doesn't she? In many cases, it is because such individuals are bonded. Some call it a "soul tie." Although this type of bonding can't be fully explained, there is little question that it is happening all over the world.

There are no guarantees that you will never be sexually violated in your lifetime, but you don't have to remain a victim forever. You can renounce that sexual use of your body with the other person, ask God to break that bond, and then commit your body to God as a living sacrifice. For the sake of your own freedom and relationship with God, you need to forgive that person who violated you. (See the Steps to Freedom in Christ for a complete process.)

People are deceived if they think they can sin sexually and suffer no eternal consequences. Secret sin on earth is open scandal in heaven. Establishing the concept of "adults only" in America led to the belief that there is a different

100

moral standard for adults than there is for children, which is not true. If something is morally wrong for children, it is morally wrong for adults.

In 1 Corinthians 6:9–20, what error did Paul need to correct in some of the Corinthian church members' thinking?

_____

_____

_____

What kind of internal conflict do you think would arise if a believer, who is one spirit with God, unites with another in a way that forms an immoral bond?

_____

_____

_____

Generally speaking, in what three ways are the entrapments of sexual sin manifested?

_____

_____

_____

If you are a victim of sexual sin, what steps do you need to take to ensure that you do not forever remain a victim?

_____

_____

_____

Are there any immoral sexual bonds that you need to break? What will you do to gain freedom from that bondage?

_____

_____

_____

What Paul says here obviously applies to the murderer, the covetous person and the extortioner equally well. But as it was not possible to mention anything worse than fornication, Paul magnifies the crime by saying that in fornication the entire body is defiled. It is a sin against one's own self in a way that the others are not.

John Chrysostom (AD 347–407)

5

Sin Dwelling in You

Romans 7:14–25

Key Point

Jesus Christ will set us free from the sin that dwells within us.

Key Verses

What a wretched man I am! Who will rescue me from this body that is subject to death? Thanks be to God, who delivers me through Jesus Christ our Lord!

Romans 7:24–25

In Romans 7:14–25, Paul reveals the struggle we have with the sin that is dwelling within us. In verse 14, he uses the phrase "I am" to imply that he is talking about his present Christian experience. His statement that he agrees with the law of God (see verse 16) and delights in God's law in his inner being (see verse 22) reveals his status as a true believer. Natural people don't joyfully concur with the law of God in their inner person nor agree that the law is good. Every disposition of Paul's heart—his mind, will, and emotion—is directed toward God. The passage illustrates that human effort to fulfill the law is powerless to overcome the sin that dwells within us. Taking into account the larger context, the passage also illustrates what it would be like if we allowed sin to reign in our mortal bodies (see Romans 6:12).

Paul knows what is right and wants to do what is right, but for some reason he cannot (see Romans 7:15–16). That is bondage, but he isn't the only contestant in this battle. "So now, no longer am I the one doing it, but sin which dwells in me. For I know that nothing good dwells in me, that is, in my flesh; for the willing is present in me, but the doing of the good is not" (verses 17–18 NASB). Paul is not saying he is no good; he is saying that nothing good dwells in him. It's like having a sliver in his finger. It is a "no good" thing dwelling in Paul, but it is not him. He separates himself from the sin, even though it is his responsibility to keep sin from reigning in his mortal body (see Romans 6:12). Evil is right there with him (see Romans 7:21), but he is not calling himself evil.

Even though Paul feels wretched (miserable, not sinful), he inwardly delights in God's law (see verse 22). True believers may likewise feel defeated and discouraged, because they are not seeing the victory, but they know what is right in the inner person. The problem is that the law of sin is at work in their physical body and is waging war against the law of the mind. The battle is in the mind.

The present-day struggle with eating disorders illustrates this mental battle. Eating disorders (anorexia and bulimia) have little to do with food; the problem is one of deception. Those who struggle with eating disorders are obsessed with their bodies and their appearance. They believe there is evil present in them, but they are deceived as to what it is. They take laxatives to defecate, they binge and purge, or they cut themselves, but that will not resolve the evil that is present in them. To win the battle for their minds, they need to renounce the lie that these acts are a means of cleansing themselves and trust only in the cleansing work of Christ.

Who can rescue us from our bodies of death if we are losing the battle for our minds and using our bodies as instruments of unrighteousness? Jesus will! He came to set the captives free and bind up the brokenhearted. Renouncing the sinful uses of our bodies and then submitting them to God as living sacrifices lays the foundation for the transformation that comes from the renewing of our minds.

Whose responsibility is it that sin not be allowed to reign (rule) in us?

MINE

What is the difference between sin that dwells in us and ourselves? In other words, what is the difference between *having* sin and *being* sin?

Where is the battle? How does that reveal what the answer is?

How can you separate who you are in Christ from the sin that may be dwelling in you?

How can you personally rid yourself from the sin that may be dwelling within you?

_____

_____

_____

Man can agree that what the law commands is good; he can say that it naturally pleases him and that he wants to do it. But in spite of all that, the power and the strength to carry out his wishes is lacking because he is so oppressed by the power of sin that he cannot go where he wants nor can he make contrary decisions, because another power is in control of him. For man is burdened by his habit of sinning and succumbs to sin more readily than to the law, which he knows teaches what is good. For if he wants to do what is good, habit backed by the enemy prevents him.

Ambrosiaster (written c. AD 366–384)

Overcoming Chemical Addiction

The saloon is called a bar . . .
It is more than that by far!
It's a bar to heaven, a door to hell,
Whoever named it, named it well.
A bar to manliness and wealth;
A door to want and broken health.
A bar to honor, pride, and fame;
A door to grief, and sin and shame.
A bar to hope, a bar to prayer;
A door to darkness and despair.
A bar to an honored, useful life;
A door to brawling, senseless strife.
A bar to all that's true and brave;
A door to every drunkard's grave.
A bar to joys that home imparts;

A door to tears and aching hearts.
A bar to heaven, a door to hell;
Whoever named it, named it well.

—Written by a prison inmate

Daily Readings

1. Understanding Chemical Addiction	Proverbs 23:29–35
2. Freedom From Addiction	Titus 3:1–15
3. Overcomer's Covenant	Revelation 21:6–8
4. Discipline Yourself for Godliness	Daniel 1:1–21
5. Accountability	1 Thessalonians 2:5–12

1

Understanding Chemical Addiction

Proverbs 23:29–35

Key Point

Turning to drugs and alcohol arrests mental, emotional, and spiritual development, but turning to Christ brings healing and restoration.

Key Verse

Wine is a mocker and beer a brawler; whoever is led astray by them is not wise.

Proverbs 20:1

Some people "linger over wine" (Proverbs 23:30) because they want to get rid of their inhibitions so they can party. Others turn to alcohol and drugs as a means of coping. Some rely on chemicals to give them some relief from their physical and emotional pain. When they feel the pain, they reach for the pills.

People feel down, so they do something to pick themselves up. They feel stressed out, so they do something to calm themselves down. It worked

The Addiction Cycle

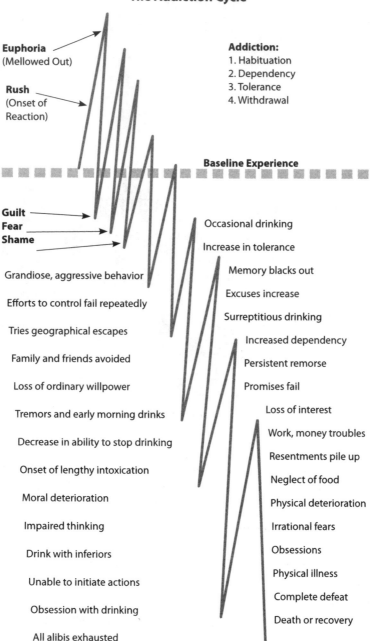

Euphoria
(Mellowed Out)

Rush
(Onset of
Reaction)

Addiction:
1. Habituation
2. Dependency
3. Tolerance
4. Withdrawal

Baseline Experience

Guilt
Fear
Shame

Occasional drinking

Increase in tolerance

Grandiose, aggressive behavior

Memory blacks out

Efforts to control fail repeatedly

Excuses increase

Tries geographical escapes

Surreptitious drinking

Family and friends avoided

Increased dependency

Loss of ordinary willpower

Persistent remorse

Tremors and early morning drinks

Promises fail

Decrease in ability to stop drinking

Loss of interest

Work, money troubles

Onset of lengthy intoxication

Resentments pile up

Moral deterioration

Neglect of food

Impaired thinking

Physical deterioration

Drink with inferiors

Irrational fears

Unable to initiate actions

Obsessions

Obsession with drinking

Physical illness

Complete defeat

All alibis exhausted

Death or recovery

before, so it will work again. Many people have trained themselves to depend on chemicals to pick them up, to stop the pain, to soothe the nerves, and to feel good. Chemical users feel the rush of the onset reaction and mellow out. However, the resulting euphoric experience doesn't last. When the effects wear off, their guilt, fear, and shame become more and more pronounced with each successive use. Their occasional use soon becomes a habit and a means of coping.

Some may choose to drink surreptitiously because they feel guilty about their behavior. Their shame drives them to leave their familiar surroundings and drink or use where no one knows them. Over time, it takes more and more alcohol or a greater fix to reach the original high, and with the habit comes a greater tolerance for the drug of choice. Greater consumption will never get users back to their first euphoric experience.

The lows keep getting lower and lower when the effects of the drug wear off. No matter what drug they try or how often they use, it's never enough. For chemical addicts, the loss of control robs them of their ability to live responsible lives. Financial problems develop as they struggle to support their habit.

The user's downward spiral of addiction leads them to greater immorality, and their sense of worth plummets. They perceive themselves as disgusting. Their eating and grooming habits deteriorate, as does their health. The vast majority of chemical abusers are also sexually addicted, and most recovery programs won't deal with that issue. They withdraw socially, for they do not want their weaknesses to be seen. They fear being publicly humiliated or exposed.

Users often become paranoid about people looking at them or talking about them. They have no mental peace. Condemning thoughts haunt them day and night. They begin to hallucinate (see Proverbs 23:33). The only way for them to silence the voices is to continue drinking or continue using. Solomon describes the numbness of those who hit the bottom: "'They hit me,' you will say, 'but I'm not hurt! They beat me, but I don't feel it! When will I wake up so I can find another drink?'" (verse 35).

Those who think they can stop drinking or using can only prove it to themselves by actually stopping the behavior. If they find that they can't stop, then they know they need a power greater than themselves. This is why admitting you have a problem is the first step in overcoming any addiction. In Christ you have power over sin, and He alone has the capacity to meet all your needs.

What are some of the reasons that people turn to chemical substances?

_____

_____

_____

People develop a tolerance to their drugs of choice, which is why larger doses are increasingly necessary to have the same effect. What is the logical conclusion of greater usage? Do you think chemical users understand that?

_____

_____

_____

Are substance abusers the only ones who suffer? What are some of the many ways that children and spouses are affected by chemical abuse?

_____

_____

_____

How can you know when you or others have lost control of your life? (Take the test on the next page.)

_____

_____

_____

Why is admitting you have a problem the first step in overcoming any addiction? Why is it so hard to admit that?

_____

_____

What Peter is saying [in 1 Peter 4:3–4] is this: We must depart from the evil deeds of pagan life and not go back to our old ways nor imitate those who have relapsed into debauchery and drunkenness. . . . These people are surprised and put off when they see us turning toward what is good rather than going along with them. And not only do they not seek the good, they fall away even into blasphemy.

Severus of Antioch (AD 465–538)

Are You Chemically Addicted?

How can you know when you have lost control of your life? To determine the answer, check yes or no to each of the questions listed below.

Yes	No	
☐	☐	1. Do you lose time from work due to drinking?
☐	☐	2. Is drinking making your home life unhappy?
☐	☐	3. Do you drink because you are shy with other people?
☐	☐	4. Is drinking affecting your reputation?
☐	☐	5. Have you ever felt remorse after drinking?
☐	☐	6. Have you gotten into financial difficulties because of drinking?

Yes	No	
☐	☐	7. Do you turn to lower companions and an inferior environment when drinking?
☐	☐	8. Does drinking make you careless of your family's welfare?
☐	☐	9. Has your ambition decreased since drinking?
☐	☐	10. Do you crave a drink at a definite time daily?
☐	☐	11. Do you want a drink the next morning?
☐	☐	12. Does drinking cause you to have difficulty sleeping?
☐	☐	13. Has your efficiency decreased since drinking?
☐	☐	14. Is drinking jeopardizing your job or business?
☐	☐	15. Do you drink to escape from worries or trouble?
☐	☐	16. Do you drink alone?
☐	☐	17. Have you ever had a complete loss of memory as a result of drinking?
☐	☐	18. Has your physician ever treated you for drinking?
☐	☐	19. Do you drink to build up your self-confidence?
☐	☐	20. Have you ever been to a hospital or institution on account of drinking?

According to Johns Hopkins Hospital, if you answered yes to any one of the questions, it is a definite warning that you *may* be an alcoholic. If you answered yes to any two questions, the chances are that you *are* an alcoholic. If you have answered yes to three or more questions, you *are definitely* an alcoholic.

2

Freedom From Addiction

Titus 3:1–15

Key Point

Grace is the key to overcoming any addiction, because only Christ can set us free.

Key Verses

"Let us eat and drink, for tomorrow we die." Do not be misled: "Bad company corrupts good character." Come back to your senses as you ought, and stop sinning.

1 Corinthians 15:32–34

BONDAGE

At one time we too were foolish, disobedient, deceived and enslaved by all kinds of passions and pleasures" (Titus 3:3). Our foolishness is evident when we think that we can overcome our enslavement to sin by human effort or by the strict enforcement of some well-intentioned program. No program can set anyone free—only Christ can do that. The key to overcoming any addiction is to get out from under the law and into the grace of God. Just trying to stop sinning will never work. If abstinence were the goal, then Ephesians 5:18 would read, "Do not get drunk with wine; therefore, stop drinking!" Paul's answer is to be filled with the Holy Spirit. "So I say, walk by the Spirit, and you will not gratify the desires of the flesh" (Galatians 5:16).

Before we come to Christ, we develop flesh patterns as a means of relating to others, dealing with pain, coping with stress, and trying to succeed—or simply survive. Some have turned to alcohol and drugs. Taking away their drug of choice will be met with resistance, because that has been their means of coping. They become miserable "dry drunks" with glaring needs and many unresolved conflicts. Turning to chemicals to deal with their problems also arrests their mental, emotional, and spiritual development. They mask their problems instead of finding biblical solutions and growing through the trials and tribulations that are an inevitable part of life.

Overcoming addictive behavior requires repentance and faith in God. The first step is to admit we have a problem and put our faith in God. We don't change in order to come to Christ; we come to Christ in order to change. People don't have a chemical or sexual problem; they have a *life* problem. People with addictive behaviors have a negative self-image; they are angry, depressed, anxious, and bitter. You are not going to resolve those issues by abstaining, which is why 97 percent of people fall off the wagon after their first treatment. The success rate climbs dramatically if they can go home to a good church and a loving and supportive Christian community.

Those who are "enslaved by all kinds of passions and pleasures" (Titus 3:3) need the support of the Christian community, where their needs can be met through their relationship with Christ and His body. That is why Paul says "our people must learn to devote themselves to doing what is good, in order to provide for urgent needs and not live unproductive lives" (verse 14). Their need for eternal life, identity, acceptance, security, and significance can only be met in Christ. In Christ they are not alcoholics or addicts—they are children of God.

The next step for those in bondage is to resolve their personal and spiritual conflicts through genuine repentance (see The Steps to Freedom in Christ). This process removes the barriers to their intimacy with God and wards off the evil one. Those who struggle with addictive behavior have no mental peace. They are plagued by accusing, tempting, and blasphemous thoughts. If they process the Steps successfully, they will experience the peace of God that transcends all understanding and guards their hearts and minds in Christ Jesus (see Philippians 4:7). The final step is for them to get involved in a Christ-centered recovery group or program that is biblically based.

Why do people turn to alcohol and drugs?

Why is abstinence an inadequate goal for those who are struggling with addictive behaviors?

Why is it so essential to establish an intimate relationship with God and resist the devil?

Have you ever tried to stop compulsive behavior? If so, how well did that work for you?

To what do you turn when you feel stressed out or anxious? Why?

_____

_____

_____

Paul says that a man in sin is wretched. For indeed how could man not be wretched when he has succeeded to this inheritance of sin, having this enemy sin with him, through which Satan has access to him? For Adam invented steps by which the despoiler came up to his descendants. Yet the most merciful God, moved by pity, gave us his grace through Christ so that it might be revealed that the human race, once it accepted the forgiveness of sins, might repent and put sin to death. For a man who is pardoned for his sins and cleansed can resist the power of the enemy which is aimed against him.

Ambrosiaster (written c. AD 366–384)

3

Overcomer's Covenant
Revelation 21:6–8

Key Point

A key to any cure is commitment.

Key Verse

Now I commit you to God and to the word of his grace, which can build you up and give you an inheritance among all those who are sanctified.

Acts 20:32

To the thirsty I will give water without cost from the spring of the water of life. Those who are victorious will inherit all this, and I will be their God and they will be my children" (Revelation 2:6–7). Every believer has a covenant relationship with his or her heavenly Father. He took the initiative and we responded by faith. You can make the following covenant with God to overcome any habitual sins in your life. If necessary, do it daily until your recovery is complete.

First, I acknowledge that I cannot save myself or set myself free by my own effort and resources. Therefore, I place all my trust and confidence in the

119

Lord and put no confidence in the flesh. When I am tempted to live my life independent of God, I will declare that apart from Christ I can do nothing.

Second, I acknowledge that rebellion is as the sin of witchcraft, and insubordination is as the sin of iniquity and idolatry. Therefore, I consciously choose to submit to God and resist the devil. I will deny myself, pick up my cross daily, and follow Jesus.

Third, I acknowledge that God is opposed to the proud but gives grace to the humble. Therefore, I choose to humble myself before the mighty hand of God so that He may exalt me at the proper time.

Fourth, I acknowledge that the law is unable to impart life or give me victory over sin. Therefore, by the grace of God, I choose to believe that I am alive in Christ and dead to sin. I commit myself to walk by faith in the power of the Holy Spirit.

Fifth, I acknowledge that my actions don't determine who I am, but who I am does determine what I do. Therefore, I choose to believe the truth that I am a child of God, who unconditionally loves and accepts me.

Sixth, I acknowledge that as a child of God, I am under the New Covenant of grace. Therefore, I choose to believe that sin is no longer master over me. I am spiritually alive, and there is now no condemnation for those who are in Christ Jesus.

Seventh, I acknowledge that I have harmfully programmed my mind and used my body as an instrument of unrighteousness. Therefore, I renounce every unrighteous use of my body. I submit my body to God as a living sacrifice and commit myself to be transformed by the renewing of my mind.

Eighth, I acknowledge that my thoughts have not been pure. Therefore, I commit myself to take every thought captive to the obedience of Christ, and I choose to think on that which is true, honorable, right, pure, and lovely.

Ninth, I acknowledge that I will face many trials and tribulations. Therefore, I commit myself to grow through difficult times, believing that I can do all things through Christ who strengthens me.

Tenth, I acknowledge that it is more blessed to give than to receive. Therefore, I choose to adopt the attitude of Christ, which was to do nothing from selfishness or empty conceit. With humility of mind I will regard others as more important than myself. I will not merely look out for my own personal interests but also for the interests of others.

Read John 15:5 and Matthew 16:24. What does Jesus say about remaining in Him, denying yourself, and following Him (steps 1 and 2)?

Read 1 Peter 5:6 and Colossians 2:13. What do these verses say about humbling yourself before God and choosing to believe you are alive in Christ (steps 3 and 4)?

Read Galatians 3:26–27 and Romans 8:1. What does Paul say about being a child of God and being free from condemnation (steps 5 and 6)?

Read Romans 12:1 and 2 Corinthians 10:5. What does Paul say about offering your body as a living sacrifice and making every thought obedient to Christ (steps 7 and 8)?

Read Philippians 4:13 and 2:3–8. What do these verses say about what you can do in Christ and what mindset you should have (steps 9 and 10)?

_____

_____

_____

The commandments of God are not burdensome. All those who are bound to keep them with true devotion, despite the adversities of this world, regard its temptations with equanimity, even to the point of looking forward to death, because it is a gateway to the heavenly country. And lest anyone should think that we can somehow achieve all this by our efforts, John adds that the substance of our victory is our faith, not our works [see 1 John 5:4].

Bede (AD 673–735)

4

Discipline Yourself
for Godliness

Daniel 1:1–21

Key Point

Discipline for the sake of godliness is profitable now and for all eternity.

Key Verses

Dear friends, now we are children of God, and what we will be has not yet been made known. But we know that when Christ appears, we shall be like him, for we shall see him as he is. All who have this hope in him purify themselves, just as he is pure.

1 John 3:2–3

Many recovery ministries and diet plans fail because they are based on a concept of law rather than grace. Just trying to stop drinking alcohol, taking drugs, and eating certain foods has not proven to be very successful. Abstinence is doubly hard if those in authority require a person to eat food and drink wine that is forbidden by

123

God—as was the case for Daniel. However, rather than just rebel against the king or put the king's official in a tight spot, Daniel suggested a creative alternative. As a result, the official saved face, the king was pleased, and Daniel was healthier (see Daniel 1:8–20).

The secular world says, "Work the program; the program works." There is no program that can set you free. You may, by sheer determination, manage to abstain, but you will still be disconnected from God and plagued by other flesh patterns. Trying to follow a law-based program where the goal is abstinence is like trying to get an old bone away from a dog. If you try to grab it, you will have a dogfight. However, if you throw the dog a steak, it will spit out the old bone. The gospel is a steak served on a platter of grace.

Faith-based programs focus on teaching the Truth that sets people free. No matter how serious the addiction, true believers are still children of God who are alive in Christ and dead to sin. Believers are not addicts, alcoholics, co-addicts, and co-dependents—they are children of God, and their victory is found in their identity and position in Christ. It is counterproductive to label struggling Christians with a negative failure identity. Paul never identifies believers by their flesh patterns.

To believe that an alcoholic will always be an alcoholic or to believe that a sinner will always be a sinner is a misrepresentation of the gospel. On the other hand, those struggling with addictive behaviors cannot deny their own sins if they want to experience the grace of God. The Christian could say, "I am a child of God who struggles with alcohol, which is not a disease. It is a flesh pattern that I am learning to overcome through repentance and faith in God."

Trying to discipline yourself to abstain from things that are bad for you will not prove to be effective. However, disciplining yourself for the sake of godliness will prove to be profitable now and for all eternity. "For physical training is of some value, but godliness has value for all things, holding promise for both the present life and the life to come" (1 Timothy 4:8).

Righteous people don't focus on what they *shouldn't* be doing; they focus on *who they are in Christ* and what they *should* be doing. "For though the righteous fall seven times, they rise again" (Proverbs 24:16). When they fall, righteous people don't say, "I'm a hopeless failure who was never called to walk." They say, "Lord, I fell again. Thank You for Your forgiveness. I'm going to get back up and learn to live by faith in the power of the Holy Spirit so that I don't have to fall again." Like Daniel, they also have creative alternatives they can choose when tempted to sin.

What alternative did Daniel suggest to abstain from eating food offered to idols? What was the result?

_____

_____

_____

What is the difference between law-based programs and faith-based ministries?

_____

_____

_____

What is wrong with calling yourself an addict, or an alcoholic, or a co-dependent?

_____

_____

_____

What flesh-based labels have you put on yourself or allowed others to place on you?

_____

_____

_____

How can you discipline yourself to think truthfully and live righteously as opposed to combating lies and bad behavior?

_____

_____

_____

St. Paul is plainly referring to this when he says, "bodily exercise is profitable for a little, but godliness is profitable for all things, having the promise of the life that now is and of the life to come." What is said to be profitable for a little cannot be profitable forever and cannot (of itself) bring a man to the perfect life. The phrase "for a little" might mean one of two things. It might mean "for a short time," since these bodily exercises are not going to last as long as the man who practices them. Or it might mean "only of little profit." Corporal austerity brings the first beginnings of progress, but it does not beget that perfect charity which has the promise of this life and the life to come.

John Cassian (AD 360–435)

5

Accountability

1 Thessalonians 2:5–12

Key Point

Mutual accountability takes place when there is unconditional positive regard for one another.

Key Verse

Therefore each of you must put off falsehood and speak truthfully to your neighbor, for we are all members of one body.

Ephesians 4:25

If we are going to live a righteous life, we need to be accountable to God first and then accountable to one another. We will all give an account to God in the future whether we want to do so or not (see 2 Corinthians 5:10). It is better to be honest with God now, receive His forgiveness, and live in conscious moral agreement with Him. "But if we walk in the light, as he is in the light, we have fellowship with one another, and the blood of Jesus, his Son, purifies us from all sin" (1 John 1:7). The fellowship is not only with God but also with one another.

We need to follow the Lord's example when it comes to parenting, discipling, or counseling others. If we confess to God, He forgives and cleanses us (see 1 John 1:9). If we go to God, we will receive mercy and grace in time of need (see Hebrews 4:16). The recovery process will be greatly enhanced if inquirers have at least one person who will accept and affirm them no matter what is shared.

For years, a husband kept silent about some sordid information regarding himself. Fearing that his wife would discover his past indiscretions from another source, he decided that he needed to come clean for the sake of their marriage and his relationship with God. He wrote out his confession and read it to her without once looking up. "What do you think?" he asked when he had finished. "Honey," she said, "there isn't anything you could share with me that, just by sharing it, wouldn't cause me to love you more."

Most people would prefer to walk in the light and speak the truth in love, but they hesitate for one big reason. They think, *If I opened up honestly and shared my most intimate self, what would the other person do with that information?* Loveless people could use that information against them, but those who care have four possible responses. First, they could give advice, but many people won't continue to share with those who are only advice-givers. It becomes tiresome to hear three things you should be doing and two reasons why you shouldn't feel that way. Second, they could give assurance, but just telling someone that everything will work out can sound patronizing. Third, they could seek to understand by inviting further discourse. Finally, they could be self-revealers and share how they struggled in a similar situation.

Suppose your son came home feeling sad, and when you asked what was wrong, he said, "My best friend just rejected me." The advice-giver might respond, "I never liked that kid. Next time choose better friends—and treat your friends better so they won't reject you." The assurer might respond, "Oh, honey, I'm sorry. You are a good person, and God loves you and so do we." The understander might respond, "Son, that really hurts. Do you want to talk about it?" The self-revealer might respond, "That happened to me once, and it was one of the most devastating experiences of my life. It really hurt, and it took some time to get over the pain."

Which person would you share your story with? Those who have struggled themselves to overcome life's difficulties are the best confidants, and it is easier to be accountable to them because they are more likely to be understanding.

Why is it so hard to be accountable to other believers?

What happens when we fully disclose ourselves to God? How does that serve as an example for us?

Of the four styles of communication, which are the most common? How can that become a problem for parents and other confidants?

If you had to be accountable to someone, what kind of person would he or she need to be?

What kind of parent or friend would you like to be? Why?

_____

_____

_____

Nearly all reject the weak and the poor as objects of disgust . . . nobody thinks it desirable to associate with them. But God, who is served by myriads of powers, whose majesty is beyond anyone's endurance, had not disdained to become the father, the friend, the brother of those rejected ones. He willed to become incarnate so that he might become "like unto us in all things except for sin" and make us to share in His glory and His kingdom. What stupendous riches of His great goodness! What an ineffable condescension on the part of our Master and our God!

Symeon the New Theologian (AD 949–1022)

SESSION SIX

Suffering for Righteousness' Sake

I asked God for strength, that I might achieve.
I was made weak, that I might learn humbly to obey.
I asked for health, that I might do greater things.
I was given infirmity, that I might do better things.
I asked for riches, that I might be happy.
I was given poverty, that I might be wise.
I asked for power, that I might have the praise of men.
I was given weakness, that I might feel the need for God.
I asked for all things, that I might enjoy life.
I was given life, that I might enjoy all things.
I got nothing I asked for but got everything I had hoped for.
Almost despite myself, my unspoken prayers were answered.
I am, among all men, most richly blessed.[1]

—"A Confederate Soldier's Prayer"

Daily Readings

1. Righteous Suffering	Job 1:1–22
2. Suffering Builds Character	Hebrews 2:9–10
3. Suffering Draws Us Closer to God	2 Corinthians 1:3–11
4. God's Ministry of Darkness	Isaiah 50:10–11
5. God's Ministry of Rest	Hebrews 4:1–13

1

Righteous Suffering

Job 1:1–22

Key Point

Christians may be called to suffer for the sake of righteousness.

Key Verse

But those who suffer he delivers in their suffering; he speaks to them in their affliction.

Job 36:15

Suffering is often understood as the consequence of our own sin or the sin of others and something that God allows for the perfecting of our faith. When David sinned, he felt the heavy hand of God in the form of physical and mental suffering (see Psalm 32:3–5). Job's three friends believed that he was suffering because he had done something wrong, but that wasn't the case. God allowed Job to suffer at the hands of Satan because he was a righteous man (see Job 1:8).

Believers have always struggled with the question as to why God allows bad things to happen to good people. We cannot fully explain that question without taking into account the evil influences of Satan and his demons, who actively oppose the will of God. If God and humanity were the only two players, then one or the other would inevitably have to take the blame for all the suffering in this world. That was the conclusion of Job's wife, who responded to his suffering by saying, "Are you still maintaining your integrity? Curse God and die!" (2:9).

The book of Job begins with Satan asking God, "Does Job fear God for nothing?" (1:9). In other words, Satan was asking if the covenant children of God loved Him because of who He was, or if they loved Him because of His blessings. God answered by allowing Job to suffer at the hands of Satan, but there were limits as to how far he could go. Job's three friends were wrong, but Job made the mistake of defending himself. Job's defense came to an end when God asked, "Who are you to question me, Job? If I am God, I have the right to do with your life whatever I want" (see Job 38–41). Job agreed, and "the LORD restored his fortunes and gave him twice as much as he had before" (Job 42:10).

Conservative scholars date the book of Job much earlier than the location in our Bibles would indicate. Suffering would be a continuous part of the human drama after the Fall, so the issue needed to be addressed early in human history. There are three valuable lessons that must be learned from the story of Job. First, we have the assurance that God will deliver us and speak to us in our suffering (see Job 36:15). Suffering alone is intolerable. Second, we have the assurance that God will make it right in the end if we are called to suffer for the sake of righteousness. Third, we should never jump to the conclusion that someone is suffering due to his or her own fault. Identifying with Christ in this fallen world will include suffering. "In fact, everyone who wants to live a godly life in Christ Jesus will be persecuted" (2 Timothy 3:12). As children of God, we share in His inheritance and His sufferings (see Romans 8:17). "For just as we share abundantly in the sufferings of Christ, so also our comfort abounds through Christ" (2 Corinthians 1:5).

Peter advised us not to be surprised by the painful trials of suffering but rather to rejoice that we are participating in the suffering of Christ (see 1 Peter 4:12–13). Christians may be suffering because they are doing something right. "So then, those who suffer according to God's will should commit themselves to their faithful Creator and continue to do good" (1 Peter 4:19).

What is the original cause of all suffering in this world? How many players were involved at the time?

What lessons about suffering should be drawn from the book of Job?

Why will godly people suffer persecution?

Have you ever had to suffer for the sake of righteousness? Were you tempted at the time to compromise yourself to avoid persecution?

How willing are you to identify with Christ in His sufferings?

If the road is narrow and difficult, how can it be that "My yoke is easy and my burden is light"? He says "difficult" because of the nature of the trials but "easy" because of the willingness of the travelers. It is possible for even what is unendurable by nature to become light when we accept it with eagerness. Remember that the apostles who had been scourged returned rejoicing that they had been found worthy to be dishonored for the name of the Lord.

John Chrysostom (AD 347–407)

2

Suffering Builds Character

Hebrews 2:9–10

Key Point

Suffering is part of the sanctification process.

Key Verses

For we do not have a high priest who is unable to empathize with our weaknesses, but we have one who has been tempted in every way, just as we are—yet he did not sin. Let us then approach God's throne of grace with confidence, so that we may receive mercy and find grace to help us in our time of need.

Hebrews 4:15–16

Physical pain is necessary for our survival. If we could not feel pain, our bodies would be covered with scars. Emotional pain is just another form of suffering and is necessary for our growth in Christ. We need to acknowledge our physical, mental, and emotional pain and take corrective steps—or our chances of survival are going to decrease. Suffering will certainly get our attention, as it should. Someone once said, "Small trials often make us beside ourselves, but great trials bring us back to ourselves."

Jesus is the greatest example of the reality that suffering is part of the sanctifying process. Apart from the suffering He endured to pay the consequences of our sin, suffering was part of His physical maturation. Scripture says His humanity was made perfect through suffering (see Hebrews 2:9–10). "Son though he was, he learned obedience from what he suffered" (Hebrews 5:8). These verses do not suggest that Jesus was disobedient or sinful, but they do imply His dual nature—referring to His growth from infancy to adulthood after He took on the form of a man.

Jesus' growth experience through suffering made Him a compassionate high priest who could identify with suffering humanity and come to their aid. The suffering of Jesus teaches us the fullness of what it means to obey our heavenly Father, no matter what the cost. We learn the chain of moral values that develop as a result of adversity. "We also glory in our suffering, because we know that suffering produces perseverance; perseverance, character; and character, hope" (Romans 5:3–4).

Jesus said, "Whoever wants to be my disciple must deny themselves and take up their cross and follow me. For whoever wants to save their life will lose it, but whoever loses their life for me will find it" (Matthew 16:24–25). The process of putting off the old self is painful. Denying ourselves is not easy, and there is no painless way for us to die. To surrender our right to self-govern—which we have stubbornly claimed as our right—is a painful process. Growth pains are an inevitable part of life.

It all seems so sacrificial, but what are you really sacrificing? You are sacrificing the temporal in order to gain the eternal. Those who seek to find their purpose and meaning in their natural life will lose it all when they physically die. Those who find their life in Christ will have the pleasures of eternal life now and for all eternity. You are sacrificing the pleasure of things to gain the pleasures of life. What would you exchange for love, joy, peace, patience, and the other fruit of the Spirit? Why would you seek to be happy as animals when you could be blessed as a child of God?

Denying ourselves is the central teaching of all four gospels, but John's introduction to the message is different: "The hour has come for the Son of Man to be glorified. Very truly I tell you, unless a kernel of wheat falls to the ground and dies, it remains only a single seed. But if it dies, it produces many seeds" (John 12:23–24). The seed can exist on its own for some time, but it will eventually pass away without bearing any fruit. The seed can also fulfill its intended purpose of multiplying itself, but it would have to give up its self-centered existence.

Why are physical and emotional pain necessary for our survival and our growth in Christ?

_____

_____

_____

How does Jesus' example reveal that suffering is necessary to perfect our character and fulfill our purpose for being here?

_____

_____

_____

"For we do not have a high priest who is unable to empathize with our weaknesses" (Hebrews 4:15). Of what profit is that to us?

_____

_____

_____

Have you attempted to live godly in Christ Jesus, and then come to a choice of identifying with Him or compromising your faith to avoid persecution? If so, how well did you do?

_____

_____

_____

Why should you be willing to persevere through trials and tribulations?

_____

_____

_____

Endurance produces character, which contributes in some measure to the things which are to come because it gives power to the hope which is within us. Nothing encourages a man to hope for blessing more than the strength of a good character. No one who has led a good life worries about the future. . . . Does our good really lie in hope? Yes, but not in human hopes, which often vanish and leave only embarrassment behind. Our hope is in God and is therefore sure and immovable.

John Chrysostom (AD 347–407)

3

Suffering Draws Us Closer to God

2 Corinthians 1:3–11

Key Point

The will of God will not take us where the grace of God cannot sustain us.

Key Verses

For just as we share abundantly in the sufferings of Christ, so also our comfort abounds through Christ. If we are distressed, it is for your comfort and salvation; if we are comforted, it is for your comfort, which produces in you patient endurance of the same sufferings we suffer.

2 Corinthians 1:5–6

We compromise our love for God when we become too attached to the temporal things of this world. Suffering helps to strip away any pretense in our relationship with God. It weans us from all that is not God so that we might learn to love our heavenly Father for who He is. Augustine said, "God wants to give us something, but cannot, because our hands are full—there's nowhere for him to put it." Suffering empties our hands so that God can give us the true treasure of life. God knows that the joy of life can only be found in Him, but we may not seek Him as long as we think happiness can be found another way. If our own natural lives remain pleasant, there is no felt reason to surrender them. Suffering makes our own natural lives less agreeable.

We live in a world of moral conflict. The battle between good and evil has brought a suffering that even God shares. He suffers because of what sin has done to His creation. Isaiah said, "In all their distress he too was distressed" (63:9). We would not know this reality of evil and the true nature of God's love for us except through the experience of suffering. The only way in which moral evil can enter into the consciousness of the morally good is in the form of suffering. A person who is both evil and happy has no understanding that his or her actions are not in accord with the moral laws of the universe.

Suffering has a way of binding people together. It provides opportunities for us to minister to each other, and this ministry serves to bring people together and promote unity among believers. This is what Jesus prayed for in John 17:20–21: "I pray also . . . that all of them may be one, Father, just as you are in me and I am in you." Paul states, "The Father of compassion and the God of all comfort . . . comforts us in all our troubles, so that we can comfort those in any trouble with the comfort we ourselves receive from God" (2 Corinthians 1:3–4).

In the midst of suffering it is helpful to keep three principles in mind. First, God is always in control of our suffering. We may never know the full reasons for all the sufferings we endure, but we know that God will use our sufferings for our own good and the good of His kingdom. God always has a purpose for what He does and allows.

Second, God limits the amount of suffering He allows us to endure. For instance, Satan could not touch Job's life (see Job 1:12). Some saints such as Job and Paul obviously have broader shoulders that enable them to suffer more for righteousness' sake.

Third, God's presence will enable us to withstand the pressure of suffering if we turn to Him. Therefore, "Cast your cares on the LORD and he will sustain you; he will never let the righteous be shaken" (Psalm

55:22). He may not remove us from suffering until His perfect will is accomplished. The will of God will not take us where the grace of God cannot sustain us.

How do the sufferings in this fallen world draw people to Christ?

_____

_____

_____

How does suffering unite the church and provide opportunities for members to care for one another?

_____

_____

_____

What three principles should we always keep in mind in regard to suffering?

_____

_____

_____

Have trials and tribulations brought you closer to God or caused you to question Him? Explain.

_____

_____

_____

_____

Why do you think proven character results in hope?

---

*Hope does not let us down, even though we are considered by
evil people to be stupid and naïve because we believe in things
which are impossible in this world. For we have in us the pledge
of God's love through the Holy Spirit, who has been given to us.*

Ambrosiaster (written c. AD 366–384)

4

God's Ministry
of Darkness

Isaiah 50:10–11

Key Point

Never doubt in darkness what God has clearly shown you in the light.

Key Verse

I form the light and create darkness, I bring prosperity and create disaster; I, the
Lord, do all these things.

Isaiah 45:7

According to Isaiah 50:10–11, servants who fear the Lord and are obedient to Him may find themselves walking in the dark. Isaiah is not talking about the darkness of sin; rather, he is talking about the darkness of uncertainty. In the light we can know who our friends and our enemies are, and the path before us is clear—as are the obstacles. It is easy to walk in the light, but in the dark every natural instinct tells us to sit down or drop out.

God called Abraham out of Ur to the Promised Land, and there He made a covenant with him (see Genesis 12:1–3). God said He would bless Abraham and make his descendants "as numerous as the stars in the sky and as the sand on the seashore" (22:7). Abraham proceeded to live as though God's Word was true, but then came years of darkness. So many years went by that Abraham's barren wife aged beyond the childbearing years. So, Abraham thought he would help God fulfill His covenant by creating his own light. Sarah, his wife, supplied the match by encouraging Abraham to sleep with Hagar, her maidservant (see Genesis 16:1–9). That act of adultery resulted in two races of people, Arab and Jew. To this day, the whole world lies down in torment.

The natural tendency during these times of darkness—when we don't see things God's way—is to do things our way. According to Isaiah, when we create our own light, God allows it, and misery follows it. In Exodus 1–2, while other innocent babies were being slaughtered, God ensured the safety and protection of Moses. God's plan was to use Moses to set His people free. Years later, Moses' heart was burdened for his people. He pulled out his sword, killed a man, and was exiled to the backside of the desert. Moses walked in darkness for forty years before God turned on the light in the form of a burning bush (see Exodus 2–3).

During times of darkness and doubt, Isaiah admonishes us to keep on walking by faith in the light of previous revelation. We must never doubt in darkness what God has clearly revealed in the light and be mindful that it is often the darkest before the dawn. When you are inclined to believe the night will never end, remember the words of Isaiah: "Someone calls to me from Seir, 'Watchman, what is left of the night? Watchman, what is left of the night?' The watchman replies, 'Morning is coming, but also the night'" (Isaiah 21:11–12).

No matter how dark the night or how despairing the circumstances, morning comes. When you can't find a job, morning comes. When trials threaten to overwhelm you, morning comes. You face every hurdle with the assurance that "this too will pass," because morning comes. Don't create your own light, and avoid making major decisions when you are down. God's ministry of darkness is a lesson in trust. We learn to rely on Him during the hard times. Thank God for mountaintop experiences, but growth takes place in the valleys.[1]

Why does God create times of darkness?

_____

_____

_____

What should we do and what shouldn't we do during times of darkness?

_____

_____

_____

Why is it so important to believe that "morning comes"?

_____

_____

_____

Have you ever created your own light instead of waiting on God, or been tempted to do so? If so, how did that work out?

_____

_____

_____

Do you believe that "morning will come" no matter how dark the night? What hope does that give you?

_____

_____

_____

We have not yet seen the things that we were promised, but we live in hope. What we see is not hoped for, but we own it if it belongs to us. Christians have no hope in what can be seen, for we have been promised not what is present but what is to come in the future.

Pelagius (AD 390–418)

5

God's Ministry of Rest

Hebrews 4:1–13

Key Point

Biblical rest is living God's way by faith empowered by His presence.

Key Verse

My soul finds rest in God; my salvation comes from him. Truly he is my rock and my salvation; he is my fortress, I will never be shaken.

Psalm 62:1–2

Moses had no small task ahead of him. He had led the Israelites out of bondage in Egypt, but now he had the overwhelming task of leading them through the wilderness to the Promised Land. God guided them with a cloud by day and a pillar of fire by night, and He supplied manna from heaven for their nourishment. However, the desert was stark, and there were no modern-day camping accommodations for five million people who would eventually wander the desert for forty years!

149

Moses, realizing the enormity of the task, had two requests of God: "You have been telling me, 'Lead these people,' but you have not let me know whom you will send with me," and, "If you are pleased with me, teach me your ways" (Exodus 33:12–13). Those are the two most critical issues in every Christian's journey. The Lord replied, "My Presence will go with you, and I will give you rest" (verse 14).

Guiding five million complaining people across a barren desert for forty years is not anybody's idea of a rest. A dog may appreciate the same meal every day, but most people don't! The only way to determine the quality of rest is to ask how you feel at the end. It was said of Moses forty years later, when he looked into the Promised Land, "Moses was a hundred and twenty years old when he died, yet his eyes were not weak nor his strength gone" (Deuteronomy 34:7). God had given Moses rest! Biblical rest is neither a cessation of labor nor the abdication of responsibility. Biblical rest is living God's way by faith empowered by His presence. The alternative is to live our way in our own strength, which leads to burnout.

Under the Old Covenant, God provided rest for His people by setting aside one day per week when no work was to be done (see Exodus 20:8–11). Even the land was to lie dormant every seventh year (see Leviticus 25:1–7). This need for rest is still necessary for our bodies, but the Law was a shadow of something far greater to come. In Christ we find rest for our souls. Jesus said, "Come to me, all you who are weary and burdened, and I will give you rest" (Matthew 11:28). Jesus is inviting us to come into His presence and learn from Him. We will find rest for our souls because His ways are not hard and His burden is light (see Matthew 11:29–30).

"Therefore, since the promise of entering his rest still stands, let us be careful that none of you be found to have fallen short of it. For we also have had the good news proclaimed to us. . . . Now we who have believed enter that rest" (Hebrews 4:1–3). God's work is finished, and we have the privilege to rest in the finished work of Christ. If you find yourself huffing and puffing your way into burnout, consider these words: "There remains, then, a Sabbath-rest for the people of God; for anyone who enters God's rest also rests from their works, just as God did from his. Let us, therefore, make every effort to enter that rest" (verses 9–11).

What two requests did Moses make of God when faced with the enormity of the task before him?

_____

_____

_____

What is biblical rest? How is that different from leisure?

_____

_____

_____

Why do so many people in ministry burn out?

_____

_____

_____

How can you personally enter into God's rest?

_____

_____

_____

How can you prioritize your life so as to avoid burnout?

_____

_____

_____

This is the work of true "rest"; namely, not having to run again to the old things while enduring transition and change. For just as God is said to rest from His creation of the world, having completed its foundation, so it is fitting that also the one who has entered "into rest" not run back again to old things, viewing with contempt the labors required by the law's virtuous ordinances to restrain transgressions. For out of necessity change and a removal from the old institution follows these things.

Theodore of Mopsuestia (AD 350–428)

Leader's Tips

The following are some guidelines for leaders to follow when using the VICTORY SERIES studies with a small group. Generally, the ideal size for a group is between 10 and 20 people, which is small enough for meaningful fellowship but large enough for dynamic group interaction. It is typically best to stop opening up the group to members after the second session and invite them to join the next study after the six weeks are complete.

Structuring Your Time Together

For best results, ensure that all participants have a copy of the book. They should be encouraged to read the material and consider the questions and applications on their own before the group session. If participants have to miss a meeting, they should keep abreast of the study on their own. The group session reinforces what they learned and offers the valuable perspectives of others. Learning best takes place in the context of committed relationships, so do more than just share answers. Take the time to care and share with one another. You might want to use the first week to distribute material and give everyone a chance to tell others who they are.

If you discussed just one topic a week, it would take several years to finish the VICTORY SERIES. If you did five a week, it is possible to complete the whole series in 48 weeks. All the books in the series were written with a six-week study in mind. However, each group is different and each will have to discover its own pace. If too many participants come unprepared, you may have to read, or at least summarize, the text before discussing the questions and applications.

It would be great if this series was used for a church staff or Bible study at work and could be done one topic at a time, five days a week. However, most study groups will likely be meeting weekly. It is best to start with a time of sharing and prayer for one another. Start with the text or Bible passage for each topic and move to the discussion questions and application. Take time at the end to summarize what has been covered, and dismiss in prayer.

Group Dynamics

Getting a group of people actively involved in discussing critical issues of the Christian life is very rewarding. Not only does group interaction help to create interest, stimulate thinking, and encourage effective learning, but it is also vital for building quality relationships within the group. Only as people begin to share their thoughts and feelings will they begin to build bonds of friendship and support.

It is important to set some guidelines at the beginning of the study, as follows:

- There are no wrong questions.
- Everyone should feel free to share his or her ideas without recrimination.
- Focus on the issues and not on personalities.
- Try not to dominate the discussions or let others do so.
- Personal issues shared in the group must remain in the group.
- Avoid gossiping about others in or outside the group.
- Side issues should be diverted to the end of the class for those who wish to linger and discuss them further.
- Above all, help each other grow in Christ.

Some may find it difficult to share with others, and that is okay. It takes time to develop trust in any group. A leader can create a more open and sharing atmosphere by being appropriately vulnerable himself or herself. A good leader doesn't have all the answers and doesn't need to for this study. Some questions raised are extremely difficult to answer and have been puzzled over for years by educated believers. We will never have all the answers to every question in this age, but that does not preclude discussion over eternal matters. Hopefully, it will cause some to dig deeper.

Leading the Group

The following tips can be helpful in making group interaction a positive learning opportunity for everyone:

- When a question or comment is raised that is off the subject, suggest that you will bring it up again at the end of the class if anyone is still interested.

- When someone talks too much, direct a few questions specifically to other people, making sure not to put any shy people on the spot. Talk privately with the "dominator" and ask for cooperation in helping to draw out the quieter group members.

- Hopefully the participants have already written their answers to the discussion questions and will share that when asked. If most haven't come prepared, give them some time to personally reflect on what has been written and the questions asked.

- If someone asks a question that you don't know how to answer, admit it and move on. If the question calls for insight about personal experience, invite group members to comment. If the question requires specialized knowledge, offer to look for an answer before the next session. (Make sure to follow up the next session.)

- When group members disagree with you or each other, remind them that it is possible to disagree without becoming disagreeable. To help clarify the issues while maintaining a climate of mutual acceptance, encourage those on opposite sides to restate what they have heard the other person(s) saying about the issue. Then invite each side to evaluate how accurately they feel their position was presented. Ask group members to identify as many points as possible related to the topic on which both sides agree, and then lead the group in examining

155

other Scriptures related to the topic, looking for common ground that they can all accept.

- Finally, urge group members to keep an open heart and mind and a willingness to continue loving one another while learning more about the topic at hand.

If the disagreement involves an issue on which your church has stated a position, be sure that stance is clearly and positively presented. This should be done not to squelch dissent but to ensure that there is no confusion over where your church stands.

Notes

Session One: Spiritual Discernment

1. Christopher Hall, *Reading Scriptures With the Church Fathers* (Downers Grove, IL: InterVarsity, 1998), pp. 24–25.

Session Two: Spiritual Gifts

1. Meade MacGuire, "Father, Where Shall I Work Today?" cited in Thomas S. Geraty, "Are We Shining or Showing?" *The Ministry*, September 1950, p. 29.

Session Three: Growing Through Committed Relationships

1. Bob Benson, *Laughter in the Walls* (Nashville: Impact Books, 1996), pp. 48–49.

Chapter 3: Sexuality in the End Times

1. J. D. Unwin, *Sex and Culture* (London: Oxford University Press, 1981), p. 368.
2. Pitirim A. Sorokin, *The American Sex Revolution* (Boston: Porter Sargent Publishers, 1956), p. 77.
3. Ibid., p. 93.
4. Unwin, *Sex and Culture,* p. 386.
5. Sorokin, *The American Sex Revolution*, p. 96.

Session Four: Overcoming Sexual Bondage

1. Adapted from Neil T. Anderson, *Winning the Battle Within* (Eugene, OR: Harvest House, 2004), pp. 12–13.

Chapter 1: The Downward Spiral of Obsession

1. "STD Trends in the United States: 2010 National Data for Gonorrhea, Chlamydia, and Syphilis," Centers for Disease Control and Prevention, November 17, 2011, http://www.cdc.gov/std/stats10/trends.htm.

2. Chris Morris, "Is the Porn Industry Imperiled?" CNBC, January 18, 2012, http://www.cnbc.com/id/45989346.

3. "55%: Percentage of Porn Movie Rentals vs. Non-Porn Movies in 2005," GrabStats.com, accessed October 28, 2014, http://www.grabstats.com/statmain.aspx?StatID=623.

Chapter 2: Foolish Thinking

1. "How Do You Get HIV or AIDS?" AIDS.gov, June 6, 2012, http://www.aids.gov/hiv-aids-basics/hiv-aids-101/how-you-get-hiv-aids/index.html.

2. "The Global HIV/AIDS Crisis Today," AIDS.gov, June 6, 2012, http://www.aids.gov/hiv-aids-basics/hiv-aids-101/global-statistics/index.html.

Session Six: Suffering for Righteousness' Sake

1. "A Confederate Soldier's Prayer," alleged to have been found on a Civil War casualty at Devil's Den, Gettsyburg, 1861–1865.

Chapter 4: God's Ministry of Darkness

1. God's ministry of darkness dramatically changed my life two separate times. The first led to my appointment to teach at Talbot School of Theology. The second led to the founding of Freedom in Christ Ministries. See Neil T. Anderson, *Rough Road to Freedom* (Oxford, UK: Monarch Books, 2012).

Victory Series Scope and Sequence Overview

The VICTORY SERIES is composed of eight studies that create a comprehensive discipleship course. Each study builds on the previous one and provides six sessions of material. These can be used by an individual or in a small group setting. There are leader's tips at the back of each study for those leading a small group.

The following scope and sequence overview gives a brief summary of the content of each of the eight studies in the VICTORY SERIES. Some studies also include articles related to the content of that study.

The Victory Series

Study 1   God's Story for You: Discover the Person God Created You to Be

---

Session One: The Story of Creation
Session Two: The Story of the Fall
Session Three: The Story of Salvation
Session Four: The Story of God's Sanctification
Session Five: The Story of God's Transforming Power
Session Six: The Story of God

Study 2   Your New Identity: A Transforming Union With God

Session One: A New Life "in Christ"
Session Two: A New Understanding of God's Character
Session Three: A New Understanding of God's Nature
Session Four: A New Relationship With God
Session Five: A New Humanity
Session Six: A New Beginning

Study 3   Your Foundation in Christ: Live by the Power of the Spirit

---

Session One: Liberating Truth
Session Two: The Nature of Faith
Session Three: Living Boldly
Session Four: Godly Relationships
Session Five: Freedom of Forgiveness
Session Six: Living by the Spirit

Study 4   Renewing Your Mind: Become More Like Christ

Session One: Being Transformed
Session Two: Living Under Grace
Session Three: Overcoming Anger
Session Four: Overcoming Anxiety
Session Five: Overcoming Depression
Session Six: Overcoming Losses

Study 5   Growing in Christ: Deepen Your Relationship With Jesus

---

Session One: Spiritual Discernment
Session Two: Spiritual Gifts
Session Three: Growing Through Committed Relationships
Session Four: Overcoming Sexual Bondage
Session Five: Overcoming Chemical Addiction
Session Six: Suffering for Righteousness' Sake

Study 6   Your Life in Christ: Walk in Freedom by Faith

Session One: God's Will
Session Two: Faith Appraisal (Part 1)
Session Three: Faith Appraisal (Part 2)
Session Four: Spiritual Leadership
Session Five: Discipleship Counseling
Session Six: The Kingdom of God

Study 7 Your Authority in Christ: Overcome Strongholds in Your Life

---

Session One: The Origin of Evil
Session Two: Good and Evil Spirits
Session Three: Overcoming the Opposition
Session Four: Kingdom Sovereignty
Session Five: The Armor of God (Part 1)
Session Six: The Armor of God (Part 2)

Study 8 Your Ultimate Victory: Stand Strong in the Faith

Session One: The Battle for Our Minds
Session Two: The Lure of Knowledge and Power
Session Three: Overcoming Temptation
Session Four: Overcoming Accusation
Session Five: Overcoming Deception
Session Six: Degrees of Spiritual Vulnerability

Books and Resources

Dr. Neil T. Anderson

Core Material

Victory Over the Darkness with study guide, audiobook, and DVD. With over 1,300,000 copies in print, this core book explains who you are in Christ, how to walk by faith in the power of the Holy Spirit, how to be transformed by the renewing of your mind, how to experience emotional freedom, and how to relate to one another in Christ.

The Bondage Breaker with study guide, audiobook, and DVD. With over 1,300,000 copies in print, this book explains spiritual warfare, what our protection is, ways that we are vulnerable, and how we can live a liberated life in Christ.

Breaking Through to Spiritual Maturity. This curriculum teaches the basic message of Freedom in Christ Ministries.

Discipleship Counseling with DVD. This book combines the concepts of discipleship and counseling and teaches the practical integration of theology and psychology for helping Christians resolve their personal and spiritual conflicts through repentance and faith in God.

Steps to Freedom in Christ and interactive video. This discipleship counseling tool helps Christians resolve their personal and spiritual conflicts through genuine repentance and faith in God.

Restored. This book is an expansion of the *Steps to Freedom in Christ*, and offers more explanation and illustrations.

Walking in Freedom. This book is a 21-day devotional that we use for follow-up after leading someone through the Steps to Freedom.

Freedom in Christ is a discipleship course for Sunday school classes and small groups. The course comes with a teacher's guide, a student guide, and a DVD covering 12 lessons and the Steps to Freedom in Christ. This course is designed to enable new and stagnant believers to resolve personal and spiritual conflicts and be established alive and free in Christ.

The Bondage Breaker DVD Experience is also a discipleship course for Sunday school classes and small groups. It is similar to the one above, but the lessons are 15 minutes instead of 30 minutes.

The Daily Discipler. This practical systematic theology is a culmination of all of Dr. Anderson's books covering the major doctrines of the Christian faith and the problems Christians face. It is a five-day-per-week, one-year study that will thoroughly ground believers in their faith.

Specialized Books

The Bondage Breaker, the Next Step. This book has several testimonies of people finding their freedom from all kinds of problems, with commentary by Dr. Anderson. It is an important learning tool for encouragers.

Overcoming Addictive Behavior, with Mike Quarles. This book explores the path to addiction and how a Christian can overcome addictive behaviors.

Overcoming Depression, with Joanne Anderson. This book explores the nature of depression, which is a body, soul, and spirit problem and presents a wholistic answer for overcoming this "common cold" of mental illness.

Liberating Prayer. This book helps believers understand the confusion in their minds when it comes time to pray, and why listening in prayer may be more important than talking.

Daily in Christ, with Joanne Anderson. This popular daily devotional is also being used by thousands of Internet subscribers every day.

Who I Am in Christ. In 36 short chapters, this book describes who you are in Christ and how He meets your deepest needs.

Freedom from Addiction, with Mike and Julia Quarles. Using Mike's testimony, this book explains the nature of chemical addictions and how to overcome them in Christ.

One Day at a Time, with Mike and Julia Quarles. This devotional helps those who struggle with addictive behaviors and explains how to discover the grace of God on a daily basis.

Freedom from Fear, with Rich Miller. This book explains anxiety disorders and how to overcome them.

Setting Your Church Free, with Charles Mylander. This book offers guidelines and encouragement for resolving seemingly impossible corporate conflicts in the church and also provides leaders with a primary means for church growth—releasing the power of God in the church.

Setting Your Marriage Free, with Dr. Charles Mylander. This book explains God's divine plan for marriage and the steps that couples can take to resolve their difficulties.

Christ-Centered Therapy, with Dr. Terry and Julie Zuehlke. This is a textbook explaining the practical integration of theology and psychology for professional counselors.

Getting Anger Under Control, with Rich Miller. This book explains the basis for anger and how to control it.

Grace that Breaks the Chains, with Rich Miller and Paul Travis. This book explains legalism and how to overcome it.

Winning the Battle Within. This book shares God's standards for sexual conduct, the path to sexual addiction, and how to overcome sexual strongholds.

The Path to Reconciliation. God has given the church the ministry of reconciliation. This book explains what that is and how it can be accomplished.

Rough Road to Freedom. This is a book of Dr. Anderson's memoirs.

For more information, contact Freedom In Christ Ministries at the following:

Canada: freedominchrist@sasktel.net or www.ficm.ca

India: isactara@gmail.com

Switzerland: info@freiheitinchristus.ch or www.freiheitinchristus.ch

United Kingdom: info@ficm.org.uk or www.ficm.org.uk

United States: info@ficm.org or www.ficm.org

International: www.ficminternational.org

Dr. Anderson: www.discipleshipcounsel.com

Index

167

Notes

Notes

Notes

Notes